Song of Songs

Dear Crenshotts Family

Shalom

&

Blessings,

Jeff Osa

Song of Songs

The Greatest Lover

JEFFREY D. JOHNSON

Foreword by William G. Bjork

WIPF & STOCK · Eugene, Oregon

SONG OF SONGS
The Greatest Lover

Wipf & Stock
An Imprint of Wipf and Stock Publishers
199 W. 8th Ave., Suite 3
Eugene, OR 97401

www.wipfandstock.com

PAPERBACK ISBN: 978-1-7252-7763-2
HARDCOVER ISBN: 978-1-7252-7764-9
EBOOK ISBN: 978-1-7252-7765-6

Manufactured in the U.S.A.   08/06/20

Contents

Foreword

MOST CHRISTIANS, EVEN DISCIPLINED Bible readers, have spent little time exploring the Song of Solomon. They might skim through it in the course of reading the Bible through in a year, but they probably don't understand what they're absorbing and certainly don't appreciate the Song's purpose and place in the sacred canon. Dr. Jeffrey Johnson has set out to rectify this situation. His brief commentary on the Song—The Wisest Man, The Greatest Lover—is sound exegetically and helpful practically. Dr. Jeff has filled his book with choice insights on the Hebrew text and relevant applications to the reader's life, marriage, and walk with the Lord. His conclusion alone, with its superb list of thirty "Christian Principles," makes this volume worth acquiring and studying. As Dr. Jeff affirms in his grand finale, "Christ is all I need. This is the message of the Song of Songs."

Dr. William G. Bjork
Senior Pastor
Grace Bible Church
Sun City, Arizona

Preface

THE SERMONS IN THIS book were prepared during many weeks and months in a very busy and active pastorate. They are not for scholars and exegetes, but for regular people who love the mystery of Scripture. Pastors and Bible teachers will find this volume helpful in teaching the Song of Songs.

No claim is made for originality, but the writer is deeply grateful for the help he received from many sources including the bibliography found in the back of the book.

Grateful appreciation is extended to my former flock at Tri-City Baptist Church, Vista, California, for their encouragement as I taught the Song of Songs for eight months. The attendance grew, and as I recall, we had a mini baby boom in the nursery during and shortly thereafter this study.

Also, I want to thank our Song of Songs Bible lecture class who faithfully met eight Tuesday evenings in the winter at Tate Springs Baptist Church, Arlington, Texas. Your enthusiasm regarding the study was profound.

Shalom and Blessings,
Until He comes,
We are Together Under His Wings,

Jeffrey D. Johnson
2020

Introduction

WE VENTURE NOW INTO a most perplexing and yet wonderful and glorious book about holiness, God's love, and human relationships. The Song of Songs, also known as the Song of Solomon and at times called Canticles, is one of the most difficult and mysterious books of the Bible. Perhaps the book of Revelation would be the next most mysterious book in the Bible.

The title of the book comes from verse one: "The song of songs, which is Solomon's." The Hebrew *Shir HaShirim* is in the superlative, meaning this is THE song of songs, Solomon's *best song*. According to 1 Kings 4:32, Solomon wrote 1,005 songs, but this was his best. This is the one chosen by God to be in the Bible. This is the *song of songs*, just like the *Holy of Holies* or the *King of kings* or the *heaven of heavens*. This is the *best* of Solomon's Songs.

This same Solomon, David's son and King of Israel, also wrote Ecclesiastes, Proverbs, and perhaps Lamentations. One tradition states that Solomon wrote the Song of Songs in his youth, then the Proverbs during his middle aged years, and Lamentations in his declining years. Another Jewish tradition states that this book was not to be read until a person turns thirty years of age.

God is not mentioned in the Song of Songs. The book is never quoted anywhere in the Old or New Testaments. And yet, it is Holy Scripture, and the Jews read this book every Passover, just as they read the book of Ruth at Pentecost, Ecclesiastes at the feast of Tabernacles, and the book of Esther at Purim. Based on this tradition, Jesus would have read this book during the time of the Last Supper.

This book is also read as part of the Shabbat tradition. The emphasis is that life is a precious gift from God. The husband will either read or sing Proverbs 31—"who can find a virtuous wife for her worth is far above rubies"—and then sometime that evening the husband and wife will read the Song of Songs to spark the celebration of marriage—a gift from God.

There are many interpretations of this book including:

1. An allegorical interpretation representing God's love for Israel and Christ's love for the Church;

2. A typical interpretation meaning Solomon represents Christ or God and the young woman representing the Church or Israel;

3. A literal interpretation which states that this is a true story, not necessarily in chronological order;

4. A collection of Syrian wedding songs; and

5. An anthology of disconnected songs extolling human love.

There are two main characters in this story:

1. Solomon

2. Shepherdess

Our primary focus will not be the arguments regarding the various interpretations. Our main target will be:

1. The exploration of God's love for us.

2. The exultation of human love and marriage.

3. The endorsement of the beauty and purity of marital love.

4. The examination of family relationships.

The story line, based on the two-character model, goes something like this:

Solomon owns a vineyard in the Lower Galilee near the town of Shunem. One day, while traveling through checking on his vineyards, he meets a farm girl taking care of her family's vineyard. The farm girl was forced to work the fields because her brothers had become angry with her. Her father is not mentioned, perhaps he is dead; she has her mother, younger sister, and at least two brothers.

Solomon falls in love with her, begins to court her, and eventually marries her. The book is a story/poem of their love, trials, passion, anger, and misunderstandings, as well as the journey of their friendship and desire for each other.

You will note that the reference to Shulamite, referring to the woman whom Solomon loves, has a special meaning. *Shulamite* in Hebrew is the feminine form of the masculine name of Solomon. Shulamite is to Solomon what Pauline is to Paul. So, the story behind the song is the story of Solomon and Shulamite or simply Mr. and Mrs. Solomon.

A note regarding the "Daughters of Jerusalem"—This title may refer to female wedding guests, ladies of the royal court, or simply female inhabitants of Jerusalem, real or imaginary, in chorus agreeing to the romance of these two people.

The Song of Songs, the Best of Songs—The Holy Scripture is filled with songs:

1. The song of Moses (Deut. 32).

2. Hannah's Song (1 Sam. 2).

3. The entire Book of Psalms.

4. Mary's Song (Luke 1).

What makes the Song of Songs the BEST one of all?
Its theme: *love.*
There's nothing greater than love.

According to the New Testament's equivalent to the Song of Songs, 1 Corinthians 13, "love never fails." God is love, a love that puts music in the heart. His favorite song could be none other than a song of love. God is saying through this book "I Am the Song of Songs. I am the object of the greatest love in the universe. For God so loved."

This book brings forth the dignity and sacredness of the union of love and marriage. It captures the reverence of love with holiness being the key to the mystery of love. It embraces human life at its most intimate level of communication between husband and wife. It unveils the portrait of God's love for His people and paints on this divine canvas a beautiful depiction of the Almighty's gift to mankind—the ability to love and to be loved by another human being.

REGARDING MARRIAGE

God instituted and ordained marriage.

a. God planned the idea of marriage (Gen. 2:18).

b. God made it possible for marriage (Gen. 2:21–25).

c. God brought the man and woman together (Gen. 1:28).

We may rightly say that God Himself made man and woman for each other; He made them for marriage. And we may say that God Himself performed the first marriage ceremony in the Garden of Eden.

Marriage then is a holy and beautiful thing, an institution ordained and planned by Almighty God for man's good and happiness and also for God's own glory.

Jesus Himself added His blessing to marriage by endorsing the Genesis account of the creation of man and woman for each other and the first marriage, and God's principle of marriage there taught (Matt. 19:4–6).

a. Therefore, the Lord Jesus Himself endorsed marriage as a holy and divine institution.

b. Jesus was born into a home (Mary conceived by the Holy Spirit).

c. Mary and Joseph were betrothed or engaged to be married.

d. Jesus not only had a mother, but a home and a human stepfather who loved Him.

e. Jesus honored the home and made it a holy institution by choosing to be born into a home and live in the home of a married couple.

1. Marriage is of God; it is a divine institution.

2. Marriage is the oldest human institution.

3. Marriage is honorable in all (Heb. 13:4).

SIX PRINCIPLES OF A SUCCESSFUL AND HAPPY MARRIAGE:

1. Christians are to marry only Christians.

2. Christians should have the direct leading of God about marriage plans.

3. A successful marriage must be based on genuine heart agreement of the couple who marry.

4. Those who want a happy, successful marriage should accept a Bible standard for the marriage and the home.

5. A successful marriage is built upon selfless love and devotion.

6. A successful marriage is centered on Christ.

The Song of Songs is the greatest of all love stories. This song carries the strongest of human emotions to its highest pitch of excitement, speaking in the gentle language of love—lyrically, liltingly, and almost dancingly. Words appear in this book that do not appear anywhere else in the Scripture. This book reflects God's richest blessings, for this book teaches us that true love is godly.

Studying Song of Songs will revolutionize your life and will enable you to enter into the mutual love, communication, holiness, and reciprocal praises that are part of the Song of Songs.

1

Song of Yearning

Song of Songs 1:1—2:6

Song of Songs 1:1

THE HEBREW FOR SOLOMON is *Shlomo*, literally meaning "Peace is his." You may recall that the Lord had told David that his son's reign as king would be one of peace, Shalom (1 Chron. 22:9). Therefore, David named his son Solomon or "Peace is his."

In Jewish tradition, *Shlomo* or Solomon, the Lover of Israel, represents the God of Abram, Isaac, and Jacob, the Lover of Israel. In allegorical Christian tradition, Solomon represents Christ, our King; our heavenly Bridegroom or Prince of Peace; *Yeshua Ha Mashiach*, Jesus, the Messiah; Jesus, the Christ; Jesus, the King of Peace.

Although Solomon was a great and wise king, Solomon set his affection upon a simple country girl. She was Shulamite (6:13), literally meaning "Peace is hers." Shulamite is the star of the Song. Two-thirds of the singing is done by the woman.

Verses 2–4, 7

She takes the initiative in expressing her desires for her lover's companionship and the discoveries she will enjoy when longing becomes fulfillment. She speaks of him very directly.

Verses 8–10

She prompts an answer and a song from him.

Verses 12–14

She quickly recounts her own admiration with intense symbols and imagery.

Verse 15

He then responds to her passionate imagery.

Verses 16–17

She echoes his response, speaking of their wedding chamber, their place of romantic rendezvous, their safe haven of rest and love, perhaps their opulent mountain getaway.

Song of Songs 2:1

She, being modest, deprecates the description of herself. She says she is one of many flowers in the fields, because, you see, the Rose of Sharon was a common flower found everywhere.

Verse 2

Her modesty sparks a compliment from her lover that singles her out as a beauty unique among other young women.

Verse 3

She echoes a similar compliment.

Verses 4–6

This is a song of yearning—yearning for a deep relationship with, and a glad cry for, the one to whom she is committed. She expresses her desire to be with him as she imagines herself in intimate fellowship with him being embraced by his love.

Her unbridled joy is evident as she pictures herself face to face with him. She desires his company in both public celebrations and intimate moments. And she desires intimacy with his entire person. Her yearning has the affection and admiration of the other maidens.

WHAT IS THE MEANING OF THIS FOR THE CHRISTIAN?

Chapter 1:2

Shulamite desires close contact with her lover. She is not satisfied with a distant relationship. Kissing is not done at a distance and only occurs in close, face-to-face relationships.

The Scriptures tell us that God spoke to Moses p'anim al p'anim or "face to face" (Exod. 33:11). The writer of Hebrews states that "God, who at various times and in various ways spoke in time past to the fathers by the prophets, has in these last days spoken to us by His Son . . ." (Heb. 1:1–2).

WHAT EXACTLY IS A "KISS FROM GOD"?

According to Jewish tradition, a kiss from God is a living word of prophecy. In the Christian context, a kiss from God would be like this:

Have you ever had the experience of reading or hearing something from the Bible that suddenly came alive for you? It may have felt like the idea literally jumped off the page of Scripture and you knew that God was speaking to you. If you have, you have been kissed by God!

There's nothing quite like having direct contact with the Creator through His Word. This is the epitome of all communication. This is what we were created for—to have communion with God.

We must yearn for this direct communion with God in the same way that pious Jews yearned for the coming of the Messiah. They awaited His coming and His kiss. The psalmist wrote, "Kiss the Son . . . Blessed are all those who put their trust in him" (Ps. 2:12).

Jewish scholars often quote Deuteronomy 18:18 when commenting on the kisses of God. They conclude that the phrase "kisses of God" refers to prophecy, or speaking His Word, such as "Thus saith the Lord." In Acts 3, Peter, in his profound sermon when he and John had gone up to the temple, states that the Prophet who should come, spoken of in Deuteronomy, is none other than Jesus of Nazareth. Therefore, Jesus is the living Word.

Do you long to hear from God? To be "kissed" by Him? It is His desire to embrace you and to kiss you as many times as you will receive. His kisses are life-giving. Jesus said, quoting Deuteronomy 8:3, "Man shall not live by bread alone; but man lives by every word that proceeds from the mouth of the Lord." In other words, we live by kisses from God.

HOW DO I RECEIVE A KISS FROM GOD?

Go to His Word. Read God's Word with a sense of expectancy, a desire to be kissed, and have great confidence in the promise from

John 10:27—"My sheep hear My voice, and I know them, and they follow Me."

If you are a child of God, you are part of the "bride of Christ." Therefore, when you go to your prayer closet (the bridal chamber), with Bible in hand, look up into the face of Jesus, our heavenly Bridegroom, and say, "You may kiss the bride."

Verse 3

Verse 3 reminds us of our soul's satisfaction. Shulamite remembers the magnificence of her lover's presence. When a person wearing perfume comes into a room, that person attracts immediate attention. The perfume announces the person's presence. Similarly, the very name of the beloved conjures up for Shulamite a sense of his presence.

We are also reminded how the house was filled with the odor of the ointment when the woman broke her alabaster box, poured it upon the feet of Jesus, and with her tears washed the feet of the Lord Jesus, wiping them with the hair of her head. She kissed His feet over and over again and anointed them with the fragrant oil.

Let a young girl in love begin to doodle on a piece of paper and soon she will be writing down her boyfriend's name. It is his name she finds dear; it brings joy to her heart. His name for her "is the fragrance of good ointment, ointment poured forth."

In the Old Testament, God, for the most part, revealed Himself to men by means of His names, such as Elohim, Adonai, and Jehovah. The people fell in love with Him of whom the name so eloquently spoke. They wrote the names down under the guiding impulse of the Holy Spirit again and again, this way and that. For example:

- *Jehovah—Jireh*: The Lord who provides.

- *Jehovah—Nissi*: The Lord our banner; the Lord who protects.

- *Jehovah—Shalom*: The Lord who gives peace.

- *Jehovah—Tsidkenu*: The Lord our righteousness; the Lord who pardons.

- *Jehovah—Shammah*: The Lord who is there; the Lord who is present.

- *Jehovah—Roi*: The Lord my Shepherd; the Lord who pastors.

- *Jehovah—Sabbaoth*: The Lord of Hosts; the Lord of all power.

- *Jehovah—Elyon*: The Lord most high; the Lord who is preeminent.

To the Old Testament saints, the name of Jehovah was an ointment poured forth, shedding its fragrance over all the people. In the New Testament, the saints think of Him as Jesus.

If there was ever a name that, as "ointment poured forth," shed a fragrance over all of human life, it is the name of Jesus.

His name is a *saving name*: "You shall call His name Jesus: for He will save His people from their sins" (Matt. 1:21).

It is the *sanctifying name*: We are to do all things, in word and deed, in the name of the Lord Jesus (Col. 3:17).

It is a *sovereign name*: "At the name of Jesus every knee should bow" (Phil. 2:10).

Verses 3–4

Shulamite says others love you and yet "Draw me away!"

I think of Mary Magdalene at the empty tomb saying, "They have taken away my Lord, and I do not know where they have laid Him." Then looking up to the one she supposed to be the gardener, she says, "Sir, if You have carried Him away, tell me where You have laid Him, and I will take Him away."

She did not think it necessary to use His name. His name is Jesus. You see, there was only ONE to her and that was the Lord who had saved her. She was so enraptured by Him, so desired Him, so loved Him that she assumed everyone KNEW who He was that she desired.

"Your name is ointment poured forth; therefore the virgins love you, draw me away (Song of Songs 1:3)."

Verse 4

The shepherdess has been brought from the hill country into the royal palace, as you and I have been brought from the distant country into the very presence of the Lord Himself, and how our hearts sing.

Verses 5–11

These verses look back to the time when she first met her lover and inquired of him as to where he fed his flock.

She asks, "Tell me, O you whom I love, where you feed your flock, where you make it rest at noon . . . ?"

He answers, "If you do not know, O fairest among women, follow in the footsteps of the flock and feed your little goats beside the shepherds' tents."

Their exchange is like the one between the disciple John and Jesus when John asked, "Master, where dwellest thou?" and Jesus answered, "Come and see."

If you take the path of devotion to Christ, you will soon know where He dwells. If you walk in obedience to His Word, you cannot fail to find Him.

Verses 12–17

These verses speak of communion with the King. In other words, as we enter into communion with Christ, He becomes all-in-all to us, and our heart is lifted into worship and praise.

Mary, in the house at Bethany, brought her perfume and poured it on the head of Jesus. That day, the King, Jesus, sat at the table, and Mary's perfume, her ointment, sent forth its fragrance so the house was filled with the odor of the precious oil. This rare and costly oil called spikenard was an aromatic oil that was extracted from a plant that grew in eastern India. Mary gave this oil as her "love gift" to the Lord Jesus shortly before he was executed. When she poured this upon our Lord's head, the whole house was instantly filled with its fragrance (Matt. 26:7).

Similarly, Shulamite calls her beloved "my spikenard." Her soul was alive with the lingering fragrance of his love. She could not forget him even if she wished.

This is like the person who worships Christ. We cannot have real worship except from a heart that is occupied with Him, with Jesus, the lover of our souls.

2

The Wedding Night

Song of Songs 2:1–7

In Song of Songs 1, we learned of the beautiful love story of Mr. & Mrs. Solomon. This chapter is full of passionate imagery of Shulamite's love for Solomon and Solomon's response to her. We discovered how they yearned for each other and how they desired their wedding chamber, their place of romantic rendezvous and their safe haven of rest and love in their mountain getaway. We uncovered Shulamite's unbridled joy as she pictures herself face to face with him. She yearned for a deep relationship with, and a glad cry for, the one to whom she is committed. She desired his company in both public celebrations and intimate moments. We learned that this is exactly what Christ desires for us—a face-to-face relationship, receiving kisses from Him daily. This is done through an intimate relationship, not from a distance.

When you read or hear something from the Bible which suddenly comes alive to you, literally jumping off the page, and you know that God was speaking to you, you have been kissed by God. The idea is that when you go to your prayer closet, (the bridal chamber), with Bible in hand, you look up into the face of Jesus, our heavenly Bridegroom and say, "You may kiss the bride."

The Wedding Night

Now as the story continues, we enter the privacy of the wedding night and discover the wonder and beauty of intimate union between husband and wife.

We touched on verses 1 through 6 previously, but let's look at this section from another perspective.

Verse 1

Shulamite is saying "I am just a common flower of the field." These flowers she refers to grew in the plain or valley that sloped west to the Mediterranean and reached from Jaffa north almost to Mt. Carmel.

His response to her was "Listen, Babe, compared to you, all other young women are brambles or thorn bushes."

Verses 2–3

The apple tree, shade, and fruit are all ancient erotic symbols, and erotic suggestions are what she has in mind as this is the beginning of the wedding night. The intimacy is all-encompassing. "I sat down" can mean dwell or remain. "Shade" speaks of closeness. The whole experience is described as "sweet" and full of "delight."

Verse 4

The "Fruit and Wine" ("banqueting house" literally is "house of wine") symbolize the ecstasy of intimacy. This is a metaphor for the man's love having an intoxicating effect on her. In other words, she is delirious with passion for him.

Perhaps in Solomon's pavilion were emblems of all the tribes over which he ruled, the banners making a notable showing against the blue of the sky. Shulamite had a banner that meant more to her than all the banners of Solomon. Beneath that banner, she found all that her heart desired. The word *banner* means "desire" or "intent," so she is saying his intent toward me is love.

Verse 5

Shulamite's passion or her "desire" burned so strongly that she was lovesick. "Lovesick" may also mean "worn-out" from this passionate intimacy; hence her call for refreshment to renew the activities in which her fantasies captured her.

Cakes of raisins mixed with apples came to be viewed as an aphrodisiac. She sought all possible fuel to keep the flame going.

Verse 6

Now Shulamite pictures herself nestled side-by-side with her lover in a full and satisfying embrace. She is absolutely overwhelmed at the thought of the love of her beloved, and his love overjoys her. The marriage has been consummated. The two have become one.

The figure of the bride and the bridegroom is frequently used in Scripture.

Isaiah states, "As the bridegroom rejoices over the bride, so shall your God rejoice over you" (62:5).

Paul says, "Christ also loved the church and gave himself for her, that He might sanctify and cleanse her with the washing of water by the word" (Eph. 5:22–23). Then he says regarding the divine institution of marriage, "For this reason a man shall leave his father and mother and be joined to his wife, and the two shall become one flesh. This is a great mystery, but I speak concerning the church" (Eph. 5:31–32). Writing to the Corinthian church, he states, "I have betrothed you to one husband, that I may present you as a chaste virgin to Christ" (2 Cor. 11:2).

Therefore, the delightful figure of the sweet and intimate marriage relationship is used throughout Scripture to set forth our union and communion with the "eternal lover" of our souls.

The first seven verses of chapter two draw our attention to the delight of speaking with those whom we love. One of the wonderful things about love is that, when someone has our heart, you do not feel that any time that is taken up communing with that person is wasted.

Look at verse 1 again:

Shoshana

Shulamite calls herself the "Lily of the Valleys." The Hebrew word for lily is *Shoshana*, which can also mean "rose." This particular flower may be scarlet, crimson, purple, blue, or white. These lilies thrive in the hidden place, not in town, not in the heart and bustle of the city, but out in the cool countryside, in the quiet field. This lily even bursts forth from every conceivable crack in the rocks.

Jesus referred to this flower when He said, "So why do you worry about clothing? Consider the lilies of the field, how they grow: they neither toil nor spin; and yet I say to you that even Solomon in all his glory was not arrayed like one of these" (Matt. 6:28–29).

If you consider the context of the Song of Songs, we can picture King Solomon in his splendid royal apparel contrasted with the Shulamite maiden, humble and lowly, yet adorned with a glory that surpassed the king's. She was clothed like this through no effort of her own. She didn't toil or spin to get that way. What a lesson for us to learn!

God wants us to stop our toiling and our spinning and allow Him to do a work in us. It is the Spirit of the Living God indwelling each member of His bride that makes her "all glorious within" (Ps. 45:13).

The Lily

The lily—scarlet or crimson, reminds us that we who believe have been purchased by the blood of Christ.

The lily—purple or blue, reminds us that we who believe are a royal priesthood and that we are children of the King.

The lily—white and fragrant brings to mind the purity of the soul redeemed by the blood of the Lamb. It speaks of the pure in heart, those who see God.

The lily holds water in its cup. The source of water is pure and clear as crystal. It is the Lord Himself, the Fountain of Living Waters, the same water that flowed from a rock in the wilderness that gave drink to God's people Israel.

The lily, a picture of the bride of Christ, is composed of millions of every color, race, tongue, size, shape, and age. We are a holy people unto the Lord. We are righteous. We are cleansed. We are fragrant—like the lily. We bloom where the Father has planted us.

Often in the valley, instead of the mountain, we are planted. There are more of us than can be numbered. Our very existence should proclaim, "There is a creator who has made me, who loves the world He made and longs to communicate with His creation."

This is what a lily does—they cause others to look to the Creator. This is a holy calling: "Blessed are the pure in heart, for they shall see God" (Matt. 5:8).

One other point regarding the lily is the fact that the lily thrives in the countryside, not in the city. The countryside represents peace, fruitfulness, purpose, and holiness for the believer in God. The city symbolically speaks of confusion, chaos, evil, and death—the opposite of peace and holiness. The Christian, in order to thrive, is to separate himself/herself unto Christ alone. We are like the Rose of Sharon and the lily of the valley, separated unto God, in the countryside, in the valley.

Therefore, we are like a lily among the thorns, among the rough, unpleasant, disagreeable thorns. The thorn speaks of those who are still under the curse, walking in the ways of the world, and the lily sets forth God's sanctified, devoted people, those who have turned from the world to Himself. Their fragrance is very distinct in the world.

The Shadow

The bride of Christ, the lily of the valley, looks up to the Bridegroom and says, "Like an apple tree among the trees of the woods, so is my beloved among the sons. I sat down in his shade with great delight, and his fruit was sweet to my taste" (2:3).

Sitting down under the "shadow" of the Beloved refers to the bride's submission to His authority. She welcomes the protection and the rest she finds in Him. The shadow or shade is used in the Scripture to speak of rest and of comfort found alone only in intimacy with God.

This verse brings to mind what Jesus said, "Come to Me, all you who labor and are heavy laden, and I will give you rest. Take My yoke upon you and learn from Me, for I am gentle and lowly in heart, and you will find rest for your souls. For My yoke is easy and My burden is light" (Matt. 22:28–30).

Many times the Spirit of God employs the figure of a shadow or shade. To understand it completely you have to think of a hot eastern climate with the tropical sun shining and beating down upon the traveler. Suddenly, he sees before him a place of refuge and exclaims as David does in Psalm 17—"Keep me as the apple of Your eye; hide me under the shadow of Your wings." And in Psalm 36:7—"How precious is Your lovingkindness, O God! Therefore, the children of men put their trust under the shadow of Your wings."

Isaiah speaks of "The shadow of a great rock in a weary land" (32:2).

Spending Time

There is no drudgery here. Those of you who are married, do you remember when you first fell in love with the one who is now your life-companion? Did you find it hard to spend half-an-hour with each other? Did you try to find an excuse for staying away from the one whom you loved? Did you always have something else to do so that you would not be at home when they would call you on the phone or stop by to visit? No, of course not! You would put everything else out of the way so you could spend time with this one you love.

So it is with the believer. The more we get to know of Christ, the more we delight in His presence.

Tasting Fruit

The bride says, "I sat down in his shade with great delight, and his fruit was sweet to my taste" (2:3). In other words, her bliss was complete.

The psalmist said, "Oh taste and see that the Lord is good; blessed is the man who trusts in Him" (Ps. 34:8).

"His fruit was sweet to my taste." The Fruit here refers to Scripture. Is God's Word sweet? Yes, indeed, sweeter than honey. We read in Psalm 19:10 that the Word of God is sweeter than honey and the honeycomb.

After my conversion, I would read and read the Scripture. I would arrive at the church before anyone else and simply sit there and meditate. I would sit close to the front because I couldn't wait until the pastor taught from the Bible. I poured over the pages of Scripture, what an exciting adventure!

Well, one of the "kisses" that I received was found in John 15:16—"You did not choose Me, but I chose you and appointed you that you should go and bear fruit, and that your fruit should remain, that whatever you ask the Father in My name He may give you." These words have always been sweet fruit to me because they impart a deep knowledge of the election of God, the purpose of God, and the provision of God in my life.

God has chosen you. He has a great purpose for your life. You will bear lasting fruit through Him. God your eternal Father, through Jesus, longs to give to you fruit to bear in your life.

Some of the fruit is mentioned in Galatians 5:22–23—"Love, joy, peace, longsuffering, kindness, goodness, faithfulness, gentleness, and self-control."

Fruit naturally develops on the branches of a fruit tree. Jesus is the fruit tree. When you are in Him, and are faithfully reading in His Word, yielding to His Spirit, willing to die to all that is unfruitful, you will begin to see His fruit developing in you.

Every time you control your temper, refrain from saying something unkind, bear patiently with a child or someone slower or weaker than yourself, your fruit is showing and growing.

Experiencing stress? An agricultural discovery was made in Israel not too long ago that showed that plants under stress produce more fruit and sweeter tasting fruit. "Delight thyself also in the Lord and he shall give thee the desires of your heart" (Ps. 37:4).

REGARDING MARRIAGE

Some think that a relationship is built by the accumulation of things or attempting to change mates or even adding children in order to create stability and relationship.

Solomon states in Proverbs 24:3-4 that a strong marriage is not built on what we have or don't have, but on what we are. "Through wisdom a house is built, and by understanding it is established; by knowledge the rooms are filled with all precious and pleasant riches."

Wisdom implies getting below the surface or underneath to the depths of our mate's mind and soul. Both Solomon and Shulamite desired to know each other to the fullest—physically, mentally, emotionally, and spiritually.

Understanding involves transparency in conjunction with wisdom. Communication is of utmost importance.

Knowledge means learning with perception. When we stop trying to learn about the other or quit taking special interest and care in the other, marriage intimacy begins to wane.

If you are struggling in these areas, if love and communication is waning:

1. Start now to restore your marriage.

2. Follow God's way of wisdom, understanding, and knowledge.

3. Work to change yourself.

Don't try to change your spouse. You change. The first step is trusting Christ as your Savior. If you have done that, then submit yourself to God's authority in your life and let God change your spouse.

REGARDING ALL BELIEVERS

We are the lily of the valley, the bride of Christ.

1. Bloom where the Father has planted you.

     Our cups hold water; Christ is the Fountain of Life. Let our fragrance be known throughout the world.

2. Dwell in the shadow of the Almighty.

     Let the Spirit of God bring you rest, comfort, and intimacy with God. Spend time with God.

3. Desire to bring forth fruit, such as love, joy, peace, longsuffering, kindness, goodness, faithfulness, gentleness, and self-control.

4. Let God kiss you through the sweetness of His Word. His word is "sweeter also than honey and the honeycomb" (Ps. 19:10).

3

Being Touched, Hearing Voices
Song of Songs 2:6–14

Verse 6

SHULAMITE IS IN SOLOMON'S tender embrace. How each of us longs to be embraced! A propensity that people have is the need to touch and be touched. It is said that a person needs at least six hugs a day to remain emotionally healthy.

Babies need to be touched. Studies have shown that babies who are never touched or cuddled often become sick, and, in fact, some die. People need to be touched as an expression of love. The Body of Christ needs to be tender and expressive toward others.

We need a touch from someone, especially from our God. How does the Lord embrace His own? Where are His arms today? His bride is His hand extended and His open arms. We, the Church, are His hands and feet.

A spiritual embrace that is almost as real as a physical one happens during times of deep worship—there is an awareness of God's presence. A loving tenderness is perceived through the Spirit of God. The glory of God becomes a reality. The bride of Christ senses the same care and protection during the very moment of worship that a baby feels when his mother or father gently supports his little head and cradles him in their arms.

Being the youngest in my family, I never had younger brothers or sisters so I never really held a baby until my oldest son, Stephen, was born. The nurse showed me how to put my arm under his head. I soon felt comfortable in holding him. I never dropped him. Not once . . .

So it is with God. He never lets go. He never drops His bride. She is secure in His embrace. Jesus said it this way—"and I give them eternal life, and they shall never perish; neither shall anyone snatch them out of My hand. My Father who has given them to Me, is greater than all; and no one is able to snatch them out of My Father's hand" (John 10:28–29).

Nothing can separate us from the love of God. Christ is holding us tight. When we are at our weakest, He is there to sustain and support us. Do not shrink back from His touch. Simply rest in the Lord's embrace.

Shulamite pictures herself nestled side-by-side with her husband in a full and satisfying embrace (Song of Songs 2:6). The tenderness between husband and wife here is beautiful. Solomon cherishes this woman who holds his heart.

I am reminded of Matthew Henry's words regarding the making of the woman in the Garden of Eden. He wrote:

> Adam was first formed, then Eve. If man is the head, she is the crown, a crown to her husband, the crown of the visible creation. The man was dust refined, but the woman was dust double-refined, one removed further from the earth. That Adam slept while his wife was in making as one that had cast all his care on God, with a cheerful resignation of himself and all his affairs to his Maker's will and wisdom. Jehovah-Jireh, let the Lord provide when and whom He pleases. That God caused a sleep to fall on Adam, and made it a deep sleep. While he knows no sin, God will take care he shall feel no pain. That the woman was made of a rib out of the side of Adam; not made out of his head to rule over him, nor out of his feet to trampled upon by him, but out of his side to be equal

with him, under his arm to be protected, and near his heart to be beloved.[1]

Solomon and Shulamite tenderly exchange an embrace.

Verse 7

"I charge you, O daughters of Jerusalem."

Scholars say that the word *you* and the accompanying verbs are masculine, yet the subject is clearly feminine. This suggests that true femininity had been lost. The painted beauties of Solomon's court knew nothing of restraint, modesty, or decency.

"I charge you" are words that are an oath, a pledge. Shulamite said to the daughters of Jerusalem, "Do not stir up." This means that love is too powerful, too all-consuming to be lightly aroused. (She is talking about sexual intimacy.) The point of the oath is that the young women should not spend their youth and sexual vigor foolishly.

Do not awaken love until it pleases. The Hebrew word translated as *awake* means "to entice." Shulamite is saying that these passions are not to be excited, awakened, and stirred up, until it is the right time. This is the idea of abstinence until marriage.

Another application could be this: Love can't be rushed. We can't make our loved one love the Lord. We can't force our friends and neighbors to accept Christ. We can pray for the Holy Spirit to have His way in their lives, and we can make room for Him to work.

Sometimes, well-meaning people can pressure us to move faster or to do something that God is not asking us to do. When that happens, stand firm. You please the Lord. Speak the truth in love and humility, resist the fear of man, and fear God.

We need to be sensitive to God's timing and leading in our lives. He is with us. He is working in each of us, perfecting His bride. Let us seek to please Him, to walk softly before Him, and to welcome the work of His Spirit in our lives.

---

1. Henry, *Matthew Henry's Commentary*, Genesis 2:21–25.

The woman's imagination has had full play. She has fantasized about the power, the beauty, and the pleasure of marital intimacy. In the next few verses she pictures her lover's approach to make her longing a reality.

Verses 8–9

Having called on the daughters of Jerusalem to swear an oath by the gazelle, the woman suddenly exclaims that she sees her beloved coming, leaping over the hills like a stag. To her he is virile, handsome, and attractive. The metaphor changes when he comes and looks in her windows at her.

You see, looking in the window is something that the stags in ancient Israel probably rarely did. But Solomon's looking in the window is an invitation for her to become a doe and join him. The leaping of the gazelle on the hills represents the physical play that he wants her to join him in.

Depicting his desire to see the one he loves after a long winter's separation, Solomon is seen as springing and bounding with speed and eagerness to get to Shulamites' home.

He is seen as coming with the speed of a gazelle as his eyes seek for his unforgotten one. Gazelles and young stags climb mountains and leap over hills with ease and grace, and so does Solomon, her beloved.

"Behold, he stands behind our wall." The word *wall* refers to the wall of the house itself rather than the outer wall surrounding the house. The picture is that Shulamite is within the house. Solomon, having leaped and bounded over the hills, now stands behind the wall outside and looks in through the window, gazing through the lattice.

The translated word *looking* means "to look by way of fixation for reflection and meditation." The word *gazing* would be better rendered "peering" and actually means "to peep or to twinkle," a reference to the quick darting glances of the eye and to the gleam of the eye.

While Solomon is trying to see his love through the window, he looks one time through a window and then through another in order to see her. Once having seen her, he feasts his eyes on her and fixes them on her to reflect and to meditate on her beauty.

Verses 10–14

"My beloved spoke . . ." This is an interjectional clause and should be taken as the call of the approaching lover. He is calling for her as he is approaching. Shulamite, having described Solomon's anxious approach to her home, now describes the words and content of this particular call in verses 10–14.

THE VOICE OF THE LORD

The Lord does speak to us. I remember between 1972 and 1973 when the Lord wooed me to Him. I resisted sheepishly at times and at other times aggressively. However, it was through the testimonies of certain people and finally through the teaching of Scripture that I came to know Him. With tears running down my cheeks one Friday evening in June 1973, I confessed that I was a sinner and yielded my life to Christ.

Shulamite describes him as "The voice of my beloved. Behold he comes leaping upon the mountains skipping upon the hills."

His voice brought all the music of heaven into her heart. It was the first thing that arrested her attention. She could pick that voice out of a thousand—it was her beloved's.

Truly the first thing our "Beloved," Jesus Christ, would have us remember is His voice.

1. It was this voice that Adam heard while walking in the garden in the cool of the day.

2. It was this voice that cast the demons out of Mary's tortured soul.

3. It was this voice that stilled the tempest of that Galilean sea.

4. It was this voice that caused the demons to flee into the sea.

5. It was this voice that healed the leper.

Shulamite remembered Solomon's vigor: "Behold he comes leaping upon the mountains, skipping upon the hills." The word *he* is emphatic and could be rendered as "this very one."

What a picture of health, boundless energy, and joy. He is coming to be with her, and nothing can hold him back. O beloved, this is exactly what our "Beloved," the Lord Jesus, thinks of us!

John the Baptist said of the coming of the Lord Jesus that the crooked places would be made straight before Him, the rough places would be made smooth, the mountains would be leveled, and the valleys would be filled (Luke 3:5). The idea is that if you place a hundred obstacles before Him, he will overcome them all.

1. The Lord Jesus laid aside His glory, the glory that He had with the Father before the worlds began, and He stooped to be born into a human family by way of the virgin's womb.

2. He entered His ministry in the face of ridicule, opposition, and unbelief to face Gethsemane, where Jesus prayed and sweated drops of blood and was betrayed by Judas.

3. Then to Gabbatha the place where Pilate sat on the judgment seat and sentenced Jesus before the people.

4. Then to Golgotha, where Jesus hung between heaven and earth, paying the price for sin, becoming our sacrificial Passover Lamb. There Jesus shed His blood for our sins as the earth shook and darkness fell upon the earth.

Not only did He go to Gethsemane, Gabbatha, and Golgotha, Jesus went to the grave. He was spat upon, beaten, scourged, crowned with thorns, and nailed to a cross. He died beneath the wrath and curse of God. He laid in death for three days and three nights while the entire universe held its breath. But the Lord came forth from the tomb on the third day.

We ask: Why would He do this? Why would He do this in all the enormous energy of His deity, to pay such a price for us? There is only one answer: "He loves us."

And, one day, like Shulamite's beloved, our Beloved, the Lord Jesus, will come leaping upon the mountains and skipping upon the hills and say to us, His bride, "Rise up, my love, my fair one, and come away."

4

Rise Up, O Spring
Song of Songs 2:8–14

SOLOMON, LEAPING AND BOUNDING over the hills and mountains is coming for his bride, his love, his desire. He comes to the inner wall of her home and looks into the windows, then another to find the one who has captured his heart. He feasts his eyes on her and fixes them on her to reflect and to meditate over her.

Shulamite, having described Solomon's anxious approach to her home, now describes the words with which he called her.

Verses 8–14

Solomon comes to the country after a long winter. He comes north to take care of his fields in Galilee. However, he invites Shulamite to come and join him—to rise up and dance and frolic among the spring flowers of the field. The fields can wait for another day . . . Come up hither, rise up, and come to me, my bride.

He points out to her that spring has arrived, there are flowers in the land, and it is a time for singing. Birds have migrated back and are singing. Fruit is on the trees, and beautiful fragrance is in the air.

Solomon urges Shulamite to rise from winter's slumber and toil and to rise up and walk with him through the spring. Solomon and Shulamite are now ready for the fruition of their mutual love, for the long winter's separation did not chill their love for one another.

Verse 14

Solomon pleads for her to come out of her hiding place and make herself accessible to him. Throughout this romantic invitation she has apparently remained silently out of sight, like a dove. Come out of the strong rocky places and clefts—He is saying lay aside your shyness and let your radiant beauty be known. He is saying I savor and I relish seeing you.

Notice the very word order enhances this notion of her beauty by forming an envelope:

Face, Voice, Voice, Face

He wants to see her countenance or form because of its beauty. The Hebrew word *face* translated is in the plural. The idea is that Solomon wants to see her because of the fullness of her beauty and the overpowering impression she makes on him. Furthermore, he wants to hear her voice because of its sweetness. The emphasis seems to be on her face, the first and last item mentioned.

Lovely (1:5; 2:14; 4:3; 6:4) carries the sense of fitting and suitable (Ps. 33:1; Prov. 26:1).

Sweet has a range of uses from the comfort of carefree sleep (Prov. 3:24; Jer. 31:26) to praise-filled meditations (Ps. 104:34) to sacrifices pleasing to the Lord (Hos. 9:4; Jer. 6:20). It connotes a deep-seated satisfaction.

Shulamite responds to Solomon's call and now walks with Him, and as they walk, she speaks the words of 2:15–17.

Notice Verse 8 once again.

You and I who know Christ realize something of what this verse means. Christ saved us, He won our hearts, just like Solomon, the Shepherd won the heart of the shepherdess, and had gone away, but he said, "I will come again and receive you unto Myself." Oh and when He comes, He will be the glorious king.

It was the shepherd who won her heart; it was the King to whom she was wedded. And so, Jesus, the Good Shepherd, has won us for Himself, but He will be the King when we sit with Him upon the throne. This is a promise—He is coming. The Beloved will not remain far off. His voice will precede His coming. You see, Jesus had to come first, and the world needed to hear His voice.

Psalm 40:6–8 speaks of the coming Anointed One, the Messiah:

> Sacrifice and offering You did not desire; my ears You have opened; burnt offering and sin offering You did not require. Then I said, "Behold, I come; in the scroll of the book it is written of me. I delight to do Your will, O my God, and Your law is within my heart."

Jesus after being tempted in the wilderness for forty days began His Galilean ministry. Coming to Nazareth, on the Sabbath, in the Synagogue, He stood and read from the scroll of Isaiah 61, which speaks of himself. He read, "The spirit of the Lord God is upon Me, because the Lord has anointed Me to preach good tidings to the poor; He has sent Me to heal the brokenhearted, to proclaim liberty to the captives, and the opening of the prison to those who are bound."

Behold, He Comes

The word *behold* in Hebrew is *Hinay* (he nay) which implies "seeing"—Look! Behold! See!

We see with our eyes of faith. Our Bridegroom-king is coming for us. He came in the flesh, and the world heard His words, and we hear His voice through His Word. When we see Him face to face, it will be by way of death—to be absent from the body is to be present with the Lord—or, as we read here, by way of rapture. He said He will come for us—"And if I go and prepare a place for you, I will come again and receive you to Myself; that where I am, there you may be also" (John 14:3).

Notice He is leaping upon the mountains, skipping upon the hills. Our Bridegroom, our King, comes in victory. He always comes in victory. He is a resurrected Lord.

Listen, no mountain can keep Him away from us. The first time He came, He leaped over the mountains of sin and condemnation, bringing us salvation. No sin is beyond His saving power. No family situation and no spiritual, mental, or emotional bondage is too great an obstacle for Him. Jesus leaped over them all in bringing redemption to the world.

The ancient scholars of the Old Testament say that verse 8 is Messiah and His redemption.

- Jesus met a tax collector named Matthew and leaped over the vileness of his profession, drawing Matthew into the kingdom of love and the Master's service.

- Jesus met a prostitute named Mary and leaped over her shame and degradation, transforming an outcast into a redeemed beloved sister.

- Jesus met a rich man named Zacchaeus and leaped over unrighteousness and a life without purpose, bringing joy and newness of life.

- The Lord leaped over Peter's fears, Thomas' doubts, James' and John's egos, and Martha's busyness.

Only for a Moment

The Lord not only leaped over hills, but He leaped over mountains. There was a mountain that seemed to conquer the Lord . . . it was Mount Calvary.

Upon this mountain, Mount Calvary, it seemed that the Son of God met defeat. Understand that only for a moment it seemed that Mount Calvary defeated the Anointed One.

- He was crucified. Death had defeated Him, but only for a moment.

- They took Him down from the Cross; death had defeated Him . . . but only for a moment.

- They laid Him in the grave; death had defeated him . . . but only for a moment.

- They rolled the stone over the entrance of the grave; death had defeated him . . . but only for a moment.

- Pilate ordered guards to stand watch so no one would steal His body; death had defeated him . . . but only for a moment.

- The disciples fled and hid; death had defeated him . . . but only for a moment.

- One day past, Pilate was thrilled that this man Jesus was no longer a problem; death had defeated him . . . but only for a moment.

- Day two, the religious leaders were glad this blasphemer named Christ was gone for good; death had defeated him . . . but only for a moment.

- Day three, Satan and all his grotesque demons thought they thwarted God's plan of redemption—Jesus was in the grave; you see, death had defeated him . . . but only for a moment.

But only for a moment! But only for a moment! But only for a moment!

You see, on the third day, Jesus leaped over that mountain of death. Death, the highest mountain, the fiercest enemy, was trampled over gloriously by Jesus, the Son of God, our Lord and King. Not only was death trampled and lost, but all principalities and powers are now under our King's feet.

As we wait for the second coming of Christ, we are aware of many hills and mountains all around us. Sin abounds. Economies fail. Violence erupts on every side. And the very earth quakes beneath our feet. God is saying through all of this: "Fear not, for I am in control." Our Lord is greater than any hill or mountain. He skips. He leaps. He bounds over them effortlessly. For with God, nothing is impossible!

Jesus said, "In the world you will have tribulation; but be of good cheer, I have overcome the world" (John 16:33). Rejoice, don't worry, the victory is the Lord's. Learn to praise Him and give Him all the glory due Him. Bow down and worship and adore Him for He is calling us to walk with Him. Cast your cares upon Him. Give Him the hills, the disappointments, the setbacks, the frustrations, and the concerns. Give Him the mountains as well, whether they are the loss of a job, a loved one, a home, disease, abuse, divorce, or a stronghold of the enemy within your family. The Lord is victorious.

Because He leaps, you can leap too. Just as He skips, you can skip too (Ps. 18:28–29).

Verse 9

The Wall

The idea of God's glory being partially blocked from view is not a new idea in Scripture. Moses said to God in Exodus 33:18, "Show me Your glory." God replied, "You cannot see my face . . . and live, . . . [so I will show you] My back, but My face shall not be seen."

You see, we get glimpses of God's glory . . . but mostly we see through a glass dimly. One day we will see Him face to face. We know in part, but then we shall know, just as we are known, according to Paul (1 Cor. 13:12). Like with Solomon, gazing at his bride through the windows, lattice, and wall, Jesus stands gazing at us lovingly, longing to draw closer.

However, something separates us. In Song of Songs 2:9, it is called a wall. The Hebrew word is *kotel* and this is the only place in Scripture that this Hebrew word is used. If you have been to Israel, you've probably been to a place called the Kotel, also called the Western Wall. The Kotel is the only remaining part of the outer wall of the great temple in Jerusalem. Many Jewish people believe that, when the temple was destroyed in 70 AD, the Spirit of God remained behind the Wall.

Maybe the Lord is asking us to consider if there might be any walls between us and our Bridegroom. So many things in the flesh can hinder our walk with Him. Busyness, unbelief, self-will, pride—these are some of the things that keep us at a distance. Determine to remove all obstacles that separate us from our Lord, knowing that no matter what, He will still be there for us with outstretched arms.

Like Solomon, however, Jesus doesn't give up. In spite of the wall we put up, He continues to show Himself to us. He finds cracks in our walls and makes them windows.

Notice in verse 9 Solomon finds a lattice to gaze through. This speaks of grace. God cannot stop loving us. He must have some contact with us. He finds an opening and peeks through. He is so patient and long-suffering. Jesus, even now, at this moment, is showing Himself through the lattice.

May it stir your soul to think that at any moment we may hear His voice saying, "Arise my love, and come away."

5

Walking Together

Song of Songs 2:15–17

SHULAMITE GOES FORWARD IN response to Solomon's invitation to come out and play and to walk in the springtime through the fields of flowers, the vineyards, and the budding trees with birds singing and the sun shining. While they walk, Shulamite speaks the words of verses 15–17.

As they begin their lovely walk together in the springtime, Shulamite notices the problems caused by little foxes in the vineyards. The text suggests that she begins to apply the problem with the foxes to the possibility of problems that may interfere or hinder love between them or create a tension later.

You see, foxes in the Old Testament were symbols of those that destroy. Foxes burrow holes through the earth and thus loosen the soil so that the growth and prosperity of the vine suffers. Foxes love grapes and can wreak havoc and spoil a vineyard, even without the kind of help that Samson gave them in his famous act of arson in the wheat fields, vineyard, and olive groves of the Philistines (Judg. 15:4–5). In the context of Song of Songs 2, these foxes are the great little enemies which threaten, chip away at, gnaw at, dig at, and destroy love in bloom before it ripens into full enjoyment.

Shulamite recognized that their love was new, fresh like the springtime, full of life, and great expectation. Their eyes were wide open regarding the future. Love was in the air. However, she desired that everything that might destroy or break up the life of love, anything that would hinder the growth of the blossom of this new marital bliss, be removed or rendered harmless. Hence, "catch us the foxes, the little foxes that spoil the vines" (2:15). But what exactly is she talking about?

Verses 16–17

Catching Foxes

Here she declares that they belong to each other. The one who has taken her heart, the object of her love and passion, the one she desires to be with is a businessman who owns land and sheep near her country home.

Solomon had to care for the affairs of his businesses and the kingdom. Shulamite had full confidence in their love for each other remaining fresh and true and that they belonged together. However, she pictures him as a shepherd who during the day is caring for his flock and the affairs of his business. This means that he is away from her. This was a challenge for her as she longed for him to remain with her all day long. Nevertheless, she recognized that if Solomon would remain with her and she didn't allow him to attend to his business, even though he would be physically with her, his mind would be on work.

Because she knew that he must tend to his business while it was day, she sends him away to finish his responsibilities. She lets go and gives him the room to do his work rather than selfishly hang on to him. She does this knowing that their time will come when he can give her his undivided attention. So now, one of those foxes has been caught.

Then in the evening, Solomon is to return when they can be together without the need of thinking about other matters. In verse 17, Shulamite tells him to come back to her when the day breaks or when it cools. This is the time of the evening breezes. He is to return to her when the shadows flee away or, in other words, when the sun goes down and the shadows grow longer until they disappear. This is when he is to return to her.

She also says that, when he returns, he is to return with the same speed, enthusiasm, and haste as when he came to her earlier. He is to skip and bounce over the mountains and hills that separate them from each other. The peaks of the mountains are to be the base from which he is to spring from one to another until he arrives to her once again in full embrace.

Solomon invited Shulamite to join him and enjoy the springtime, but Solomon had certain business affairs to complete, so she asks him to go and finish what he needs to do and then come swiftly back to her. Then they will spend time together as he promised her. She will not claim him for herself completely until he has accomplished all his work. Oh, but when he returns to her in the evening, she will rejoice as he will become her guide through the newborn spring.

By letting him complete his work, and thus clear it from his mind, she catches one little fox and renders it harmless. The second fox that is caught is that they are able to arrange time when they could be completely by themselves without any outside interference. A third fox that is caught is that Solomon, as a result of him caring for the business at hand, is able to leave his work at the office and not bring it home with him.

To recap verses 8–17, we have Shulamite reflecting on a springtime visit from her beloved Solomon. She describes his approach as he is leaping and bounding over hills and mountains to get to her. Nothing will stop him. To her, he is virile, handsome, and her hero.

He calls to her to come and frolic among the lilies of the field, among the vineyards and hills and valleys. Solomon says to her that spring is here and nature is in full bloom and coming to life and so it is with our love—it is in full bloom, full of life and expectancy. And, as they walk, she notices the damage done by the little foxes. She wants to be sure that they work out any little problem before they start their lifelong adventure together.

Before the love can come to fruition in marriage, she wants everything removed that might prove harmful. She did not want anything to disturb the peace of love between them. These foxes represent all the great, as well as the little, things that can threaten to gnaw at and destroy love in bloom before it ripens into full enjoyment. "Catch us the foxes, the little foxes that spoil the vines, for our vines have tender grapes" (2:15). She did not selfishly hang on to him, and she let him complete his work. She sent him away to complete his work knowing that he would return to her in the evening when all of his time would be hers.

Certain application can be drawn from this drama before us:

1. If you are courting and you discover problems, don't fall into the trap of saying "we can work these things out after we are married." If you can't work them out before marriage, you will probably not be able to work them out after you are married. If you are married and problems arise, if tension unfolds, nip it in the bud. You must deal with it immediately, don't wait. Don't let it fester. Little foxes must be caught early, whenever possible, in order to lessen the damage.

2. Allow your spouse to finish any work that needs to be done. If your spouse feels that you are interfering by demanding attention and their work suffers, that tension will come into your home. Allow your spouse to finish their work so it can be out of their mind when they are home.

3. The other side of the coin is this: You should not bring your work home with you. This is especially hard if you are self-employed or in the ministry which makes it harder to separate home and vocation. There is a propensity to bring unfinished papers home. Of course, at times, this is absolutely necessary because of deadlines and so forth. However, this must not become a regular practice. If your office is in your home, you should not bring that stuff to the dinner table or bedroom.

The principle is to leave it there in your office. This involves the state of mind just as much as the geographical change.

4. The time a couple spends with each other should be totally theirs with undivided attention. Send the kids to grandma's. Plan to schedule your activities in such a way that you can spend free time with each other. Plan, at least once a week, to have an evening or an afternoon or a day together. Spending time together will build a relationship, while the lack of spending time together will erode what is built.

The Time is Right

Another level of meaning regarding the word *vines* is a comparison and a play on the words *vines* and *vineyards* in Song of Songs 1:5–6. The reference is to Shulamite's complexion as a result of her being in the sun and toiling in the vineyards all day long. It has a reference to youthful beauty being taken away. The idea is that the ravages of the aging process can sap the beauty and vitality of people. She is saying "the time is ripe, (the tender grapes or blossoms) for love; the freshness of youth is at its prime (vines)." Or in other words "Let's never lose that freshness and expression of love for each other. Let's never allow the beauty and vigor that we feel to wane. Do not let the foxes spoil the vines. Solomon, my beloved, whatever it takes to keep love alive, let's do it. Whatever hinders our love, let's catch it and render it harmless. Let's do away with it. Nothing should come between us. Nothing should take our love away. Let's not allow anything to quench the fire of our passion."

"My beloved is mine, and I am his. He feeds his flock among the lilies" (2:16) is the formula and pledge of mutual possession.

The Song underscores the exclusiveness of the lovers' commitment to each other and the wholehearted, unreserved character of their covenant. For the lovers, this covenant pledge carries erotic overtones: They belong to each other and intend to enjoy themselves intimately.

In Song of Songs 6:3, Solomon feeds (his flocks) among the lilies. Not only can "the lilies" be a description of Shulamite's common and yet profound beauty, it has another special meaning as found in 5:13 where the lilies represent the man's lips. And yet we find another meaning of the lilies in 4:5. The lilies describe the upper portion of the woman's body, surrounding her breasts. So, in context, the lover is feeding himself in the amorous kissing and caressing of his beloved.

Bride's Passion

Shulamite, in her imagination, sketches the scene in vivid detail. She is enjoying every moment of it. She wants this moment to last forever. "Turn my beloved and be like a gazelle" probably means turn to me in the full attention that love warrants. She envisions him coming over the mountains like a gazelle. She fancies him enjoying her mountains, the curvaceous contours of her body, such as described in 4:6.

Her imagination obviously describes the bride's passion for her bridegroom. Her sole desire is to be with him.

She dreams of him . . . she longs for him . . . she desires him . . . she wants to know him and his power and passion, his provision and protection. Shulamite gave herself more fully and freely to her beloved in passionate loyalty; "my beloved is mine, and I am his. He feeds his flock among the lilies. Until the day breaks and the shadows flee away . . ." (Song of Songs 2:16–17).

Nobody can come between two who are completely devoted to each other. Nobody can come between our soul and the Savior as long as we are determined to be loyal to Him.

Shulamite encourages her heart with a threefold thought of her beloved:

1. "My beloved is mine and I am his"—She occupies herself with his relationship, more real to her than any family tie.

2. "He feeds his flock among the lilies"—She thinks of his royalty, as the lily is a regally robed flower, and his intimacy and love for her.

3. "Until the day breaks and the shadows flee away"—She occupies herself with dreams of his return in the cool of the evening.

Therefore, the absence of our Lord should quicken our longing for Him. The mountains of separation have stood solid and silent for 2,000 years. It has been so long since the Word came from glory. The two celestial beings told the bewildered disciples on the Mount of Olives as Christ ascended up through the heavens: "This same Jesus, who was taken up from you into heaven, will so come in like manner as you saw Him go into heaven" (Acts 1:11).

- We are imprisoned on a rebellious planet in a world of time and space; He inhabits eternity.

- We are creatures of mortal clay; He is the uncreated, self-existing Son of the living God.

    We need to remember that those mountains of separation are nothing to Him. One of these days, He will rend the heavens—the clouds and the sky will roll back like a scroll; they will split apart, and every mountain will be removed out of its place (Rev. 6:14). One day, Jesus, our Bridegroom, will come down, annihilating all distance and dissolving all time.

Catching Foxes

"O my dove, in the clefts of the rock, in the secret places of the cliff, let me see your face . . . Catch us the foxes, the little foxes that spoil the vines" (2:14–15).

The closer we draw to our Lord, the more obvious and glaring our sins become. It is in the presence of God's dove-like Spirit that we perceive little foxes.

The juxtaposition or the relationship here of doves (v. 14) and foxes (v. 15) is interesting. There can't be a better pair of opposites. You may know that the dove is a symbol of the Holy Spirit, and it can also be a symbol of the bride of Christ who has that Spirit dwelling inside of her. What does she have to do with foxes? She has to war with them.

Foxes do not go away simply because you have trusted in Christ. The Amorites and Canaanites did not go away when God brought the Israelites into the promised land. God told Moses, "But if you do not drive out the inhabitants of the land from before you, then it shall be that those whom you let remain shall be irritants in your eyes and thorns in your sides, and they shall harass you in the land where you dwell" (Num. 33:55).

This could be the Lord's words to us regarding the little foxes in our lives. Little foxes represent sins in our lives. They represent the old nature. They are hindrances to our spiritual growth, and we must do something about them. Foxes are sly, quick, and destructive. God gives us the power to defeat them and is glorified when we do.

Foxes were very common in the land of Israel at the time of Jesus and they were very fond of grapes. Jesus calls Herod a fox.

"Catch the foxes" or "take the foxes" or "let's take the foxes" is similar to the Lord's plea in Isaiah 1:18—"Let us reason together." Both refer to sin. Sin must be dealt with if we are to go on with the Lord.

Foxes are symbolically enemies of God and His people.

Three Categories of Little Foxes

1. The wrong we think or "heart sins"—These are secret sins, such as attitudes regarding pride, bitterness, not forgiving others, jealousy, anger, compromising, lust, defensiveness, and worry.

2. The wrong we say or "lip sins"—This speaks of an unruly tongue: lying, criticism, gossip, slander, belittling, and complaining.

3. The wrong we do or "behavioral sins"—Unloving actions manifested in our lives: where we are unkind, selfish, lazy, self-indulgent, unfaithful, rebellious, manipulating, and

controlling. If you feed these little foxes they will grow. If you stroke them or feel sorry for yourself, it can grow into an ugly spirit of self-pity. A little exaggeration here and there can evolve into a full-blown lying spirit. Little foxes are a serious business (Ps. 97:10).

Little foxes must be dealt with in an aggressive manner. Ask the Lord to reveal any little foxes in your life, and recognize them for what they are. Or, if you're brave, ask your husband, wife, children, parents, or others close to you what your little foxes are.

Determine to deal with the little foxes with the Lord's help. Declare war on them. Don't feed or pet them! Hate them! Starve them to death!

Feed the spirit, deny the flesh, confess your sin, and remember 1 John 1:9 as you make spiritual housecleaning a priority. "If we confess our sins, He is faithful and just to forgive us our sins and to cleanse us from all unrighteousness." Jesus, our beloved Bridegroom, will give us the victory over the little foxes.

Verses 15–17

Our Enemy

There is a promise of fruit in verse 15. The bride of Christ was chosen to bear fruit: sweet, luscious, lasting fruit. Little foxes love to steal fruit. Just as a little bit of leaven can leaven a whole lump, a little fox can spoil an entire vine. These little foxes creep in unnoticed and destroy vines in blossom. The fruit is nipped in the bud before it can ever burst forth in all its ripeness and beauty as God intended.

Our enemy, Satan, is interested in stopping us in the springtime of our love and resolve and commitment to follow Christ. His goal is to steal and destroy. He often does this by deceiving.

1. Satan causes us to rationalize our sin: "I'm just made that way as a person" we tell ourselves.

2. Satan causes us to mislabel our sin: We say, "I have a problem with people like that."

3. Satan causes us to make light of our sin: "The Lord understands my weakness in that area."

4. Satan causes us to be unaware of our sin: "Who, me gossip?"

These foxes represent as many obstacles or temptations as have plagued lovers throughout the centuries. Perhaps it is the fox of uncontrolled desire that drives a wedge of guilt between couples. Perhaps it is the fox of mistrust and jealousy that breaks the bond of love. Or it may be the fox of selfishness and pride that refuses to let one acknowledge his fault to another. And, it may be an unforgiving spirit that will not accept the apology of the other.

These little foxes have been ruining vineyards for years and the end of their work is not in sight. Solomon's and Shulamite's willingness to solve them together is an evidence of their maturity.

Two Groups of People

"For our vines have tender grapes" (2:15).

This verse brings to mind two groups of people in the Body of Christ. New believers and children—both groups are particularly targeted by Satan.

Do you remember Pharaoh who tried to thwart and truncate the growth of the infant nation Israel? Pharaoh was concerned with the blossoming of the Hebrew vine in his land. He ordered that all Jewish male babies be cast into the river. Moses was one of those babies he tried to kill. However, Moses was saved by Pharaoh's daughter, who raised him in the king's palace.

A story is recorded for us in the ancient Jewish writings regarding the many other babies who were not saved. According to this tale, the Jewish women, in order to avoid Pharaoh's harsh decree, would hide their infant sons in basements. The wicked, demonically motivated Egyptians would take their own young children into the Jewish houses and pinch them to make them cry. In response to these cries, the Jewish babies would start to cry and their hiding places would be discovered, resulting in their being cast into the river. In this case, the little Egyptian foxes were used to help spoil the tender blossoms of the Jews. Children continue to be the target of the enemy today because they are young, tender, and impressionable.

The second group of people that Satan loves to attack is new believers. New believers, as little children, need watchful care.

Shulamite said, "My beloved is mine, and I am his." Like a child coming home with the excitement of a new toy, she said, "He is mine! He is mine! He is mine! This is what I have been looking for all my life—Jesus is mine!"

He is my Beloved; He is my first and only love. This is true for old and new believers. To belong to Jesus means that we no longer belong to ourselves. This principle is very difficult to flesh out, but never give up.

ONE FINAL THOUGHT

Regarding catching the foxes in your marriage, Ephesians 5 gives us wisdom:

1. Be careful of the fox of confusion (Eph. 5:15)—"See then that you walk" means be careful how you walk. The word *careful* means "to do something regarding your relationship with an exact purpose in mind." And *walk* conveys the thought of "managing or conducting oneself daily." Putting it all together, this phrase means to keep on taking heed how accurately you conduct your lives. Paul says "not as fools but as wise" which means we are to have a clear, unconfused understanding of our marital responsibilities as given in Scripture.

2. Be careful of the fox of time (v. 16)—Make the most of your time. Life is short, and time is precious. Today is a gift to you from God, so use today wisely.

3. Be careful of the fox of insensitivity (v. 17)—Paul is saying "don't be thick headed!" Don't be impervious to another's feelings. In our marriages, we need to keenly perceive what

our roles are and then put our knowledge into practice. This is the idea to understand what the will of the Lord is.

4. Be careful of the fox of trying to escape—"I can't cope anymore. I give up. I am going to get involved in something else or with someone else." In other words, you are trying to run away from your marital responsibilities and difficulties. Paul is saying, "Don't run away anymore. Face them; face your problems." And when you do, let the Spirit of God control your actions and reactions.

5. Be careful of the fox of stubbornness (vv. 19–21)—"I can't stand you, but I'm not leaving. I'll live with you. I'll grit my teeth and bear it, but I hate it! And I won't change either." Read verse 21. A deep, genuine, wholesome reverence for Christ as Lord, displayed through mutual submission, will eliminate the fox of stubbornness.

Shulamite was committed to her beloved and knew of his loyalty, love, and commitment to her. "My beloved is mine, and I am his."

Those who trust in Christ can say: "Jesus is mine, and I am His." "For I am persuaded that neither death nor life, nor angels nor principalities nor powers, nor things present nor things to come, nor height nor depth, nor any other created thing, shall be able to separate us from the love of God which is in Christ Jesus our Lord" (Rom. 8:38–39).

6

The Dream
Song of Songs 3:1–5

AT THE BEGINNING OF Song of Songs 3, the scene abruptly changes from the idyllic summer walk between Shulamite and Solomon. From the beautiful hills and valleys of the Galilee and walking among the flowers, trees, and vineyards in the spring air. From intimate conversation about love, the future, and potential problems that may surface in their marriage to now a scene where Solomon apparently left for the day and Shulamite recounts what seems to have been a dream.

Verses 1–5

In verse one, the Hebrew word translated *night* is found in the plural, meaning that Shulamite had this dream for several nights. She would be sleeping when a painful longing would seize her.

In the dream, Solomon had appeared to have forsaken her and withdrawn from her, and she was unable to recover him. This dream was so real that when she awoke she put out her hand to touch him, but he was not there.

It had left her shaken with her heart crying out for her lover.

Have you ever dreamed a dream so vividly about our heavenly Beloved?

You know the night watches are a wonderful time in which to seek Him.

When you can't sleep at night, instead of tossing and turning, quietly compose your thoughts and think of or get up and read Psalm 23 or Isaiah 53 or John 10 or some other great passage of Scripture that speaks of Him. This is what I do.

In verse two, Shulamite describes her frantic search for her beloved.

Notice in verses 1, 2, 3, and 4 the words "the one I love." She wears her heart on her sleeve. The Hebrew is literally "whom my soul (my very self, my whole person; like in 1:7) loves." She seeks him until her frustration is almost at the breaking point.

Into the Streets

She runs into the city streets in the thick of the night looking for him, but she is unable to find him. Think of what this woman did. She arose from her bed, slipped out into the night alone, and began to explore the dark streets of that eastern city, driven by her heart's hunger for her Shepherd. It was a foolish thing to do.

Had she forgotten that he was tending his flocks and would not have been in the city but out in the fields? Had she forgotten the dangers that lurk on a city street in the middle of the night?

Her loneliness, her longing, her love drove her to a course of action which was not merely unwise but foolish. The woman's quest was urgent. She risked the dangers and abuses of the streets of her darkened town in her midnight search.

Six Poems

To understand the Song of Songs a little better, we can divide the Song into six poems:

1. Poem 1 (chapters 1–2:7) is a poem of yearning for each other and discovery.

2. Poem 2 (chapters 2:8—3:5) is a poem of suspense and response to love.

3. Poem 3 (chapters 3:6—5:1) is a poem of admiration for each other and satisfaction of each other.

4. Poem 4 (chapters 5:2—6:3) is a poem of frustrations and delights.

5. Poem 5 (chapters 6:4—8:4) is a poem of fantasy, teasing, intimacy, and celebration.

6. Poem 6 (chapter 8:5–14) is a poem of passion and commitment.

In Poem 2, Shulamite risked the dangers and abuses of the streets of her town in her midnight search for the one she loves. According to Song of Songs 5:7 or Poem #4, the poem of frustrations and delights, something terrible happened to her while she was searching for her beloved. Apparently, and 5:7 implies this, she was pummeled about by guardians of the city. "They took my veil away from me" implies that they may have stripped her and humiliated her.

These guards were the so-called watchmen of the city. Their main duty was not to control crime in the city, but to protect it from marauding groups of outsiders, Bedouin bands, or gangs of highwaymen.

Note the fact that she pauses neither to give vent to her feelings of shame nor to call for their punishment. This seems to pinpoint the sharpness of her focus.

Her midnight wandering may have marked her in their eyes as a prostitute to whom they felt no obligation to show common decency. We will discuss this more fully later when we arrive in chapter five. Nevertheless, I wanted you to see her passion, resolve, and focus to be with her lover.

The passage back in 3:3–4 says nothing of the watchmen's conduct. They seem to have given her question a shrug in verse 3, as she hurried by them in her pursuit. No sooner had the question left her mouth when she saw her beloved.

Verse 4

She seized him. The story does not tell us how or why he happened to be there, but he was, just when she needed him most. "I held him" describes the complete relief she felt just as her despair built to a peak. The verb "held" is identical to "catch" in the song about the foxes (2:15).

Her wordplay may be intentional: time is fleeting; she wastes no minute of opportunity to enjoy the affections of her lover. That urgency may help to account for the mention of the "house of my mother." No time is to be spared for a tryst in the woods to enjoy the balmy beauty of a spring evening. She is in town and takes her loved one directly to her own home.

The word *chamber* means "bedroom." She delights to think of having a romantic rendezvous in the very room where she was conceived.

Verse 5

She closes Poem 2 as she closed Poem 1, by putting her friends under oath to recognize that love like hers was too hot to handle, except under the right circumstances (in marriage only), and was not to be artificially or prematurely kindled. She is reminding her friends to keep pure. Abstinence is always in vogue. Abstinence is the way, whether it was 3,000 years ago or the 21st century.

The closer a couple comes to the event of marriage, the more their hearts taste it in advance. The ultimate intimacy, the complete embrace, is all the more wonderful when they have contemplated its coming and are able to celebrate it in the fullness of covenant commitment and the freedom from fear and guilt that marriage bestows.

Pity the persons, and their number today seems legion, who are robbed of the exquisite joy of anticipation by engaging in physical acts of intercourse with persons whom they barely know.

Our fast-food style of life may sustain us physically, but its sexual counterpart diminishes our true humanity virtually beyond recognition. Keep it pure, folks. If you have sinned, realize there is forgiveness in Christ. Confess it to Christ and remember what He said to the one caught in adultery—"Go and sin no more."

Relentless

The opening verse (3:1) depicts the restlessness of one who has lost the sense of their beloved's presence. What Christian has not known such experiences, such as not sensing the Lord's presence? David stated in Psalm 30:7, "Lord, by Your favor You have made my mountain stand strong; You hid Your face, and I was troubled."

When the Lord seemingly withdrawals the light of His face, it is not necessarily in anger. Sometimes the Lord is warning or cautioning us. It is love's way of bringing the soul to a realization of something cherished. It may be a testing of faith.

Jesus announced to His disciples that He was leaving by saying, "Ye believe in God, believe also in Me." That is to say, as you have believed in God whom you have never seen, so when I am absent believe in Me. I will be just as real—and just as true—although you will not see Me. Though the soul loses the sense of His presence, He still is faithful. He never forsakes His people though He seems to have withdrawn and He does not manifest Himself.

This is indeed a test of faith and of true-hearted devotion.

When the Lord as a boy stayed in the temple, even Mary and Joseph went on supposing him to be with them, and when they did not find Him they searched for Him with passion until they found Him.

In 3:1, Shulamite feels her loss. She seeks for him; he is not there. There is no response to her cry. For her, rest is impossible with this awful sense of loneliness upon her. She must seek until she finds. She cannot be content without him. Oh, Christian, would to God that this be true of us.

Shulamite tossed and turned seeking him in vain upon her bed. She wanted the communion she used to have with him, as David when he thirsted for God, for the living God. She sought him and saw no signs of him, yet she looked for him.

Where are you, my Beloved? Where are you, God? I am searching for you; please show me your face. She must find the one who is all-in-all to her. Love does not survive alone in a vacuum. Only the sense of his presence can fill and satisfy her heart.

Shulamite leaves her mountain home and goes forth in search of the object of her deep affections. To the city she winds her way and wanders about its streets and peers into every hidden place, looking only for him.

Hunger

The Lord Jesus treasures nothing more than a genuine heart hunger for Himself and the expressions of that love. However, the Lord cautions us not to do things which are foolish or which would compromise the testimony.

He understands the temptations. Satan urged Him to throw Himself down from the pinnacle of the temple in order to demonstrate the greatness of His trust in God. That kind of thing is not faith but folly.

Grandiose schemes often end in disaster. Their promoters, like Simon Peter in his fleshly enthusiasm on more than one occasion, tend to run ahead of God. It would be possible to cite numerous instances of works which expanded too fast, that branched out into daring ventures which obviously were not in the mind of God. They collapsed and brought shame and discredit upon the testimony of Christ.

There is a fine line between commitment and common sense.

One should never do anything without seeking the will of God in diligent prayer, nor act in a way contrary to the known and revealed mind and will of God as set forth in Scripture.

Patience

God never asks us to act in a way that is contrary to His Word. Nor does He ask us to act on impulse. We need to remember when we are contemplating a course of action that calls for a decision that it is the tempter, Satan, who puts the pressure on, who urges a hurried decision.

The great principle to remember when contemplating some bold action for God is the principle of patience: "Wait, I say, on the Lord" (Ps. 27:14).

Song of Songs 3:2 shows us that even though Shulamite does not find him at first, she keeps on looking. She is not driven off by the disappointment. She says, "I will rise now" or in other words "I will not lie here if I cannot find my beloved here. I will rise now without delay and seek him immediately."

Those that seek Christ must not be startled by difficulties. We must keep on, even like Jacob, and wrestle with God until He blesses us and shows us His face and His desire for us.

Verse 4

Her soul is empty. She misses him; she cannot be happy without the sense of his presence. Her only joy is found in abiding in his love.

She finds him when she seeks for Him with all her heart. God said, "And you will seek Me and find Me, when you search for Me with all your heart" (Jer. 29:13).

Simeon waited and looked for the consolation of Israel. He waited, sought, and at long last held Him, the Messiah, in his arms. He who walked in the darkness seeking and longing for Him found Him, held Him, and glorified God who kept His promise.

Shulamite then saw her beloved. The story does not tell us how or why he happened to be there, but he was, just when she needed him most.

How wonderful! How marvelous! Glory to God! Praise His name. The Lord always reveals Himself to those who truly love Him.

He has his own inimitable way of making His presence felt, of drawing close to us to comfort and cheer us, just when we need Him most.

Notice she seizes her beloved—"When I found the one I love, I held him and would not let him go."

Clinging

Can you see that scene in your mind? Her clinging to him, sobbing out her love, telling him in broken sentences all that had happened.

This is so true to life.

Remember Mary Magdalene alone in the garden on the resurrection morning, staring at the empty tomb, feeling forsaken, abandoned, and alone. Then suddenly she heard a sound and wheeled around to see, in the glory of the morning, a man standing there. She thought he was the gardener; he must have removed the body. She begged him to tell her where it was hidden.

Then the stranger spoke a word, just one, "Mary." In that moment she knew it was Him; it was the Lord. She flung her arms around Him crying, saying "Rabboni," meaning teacher, teacher. Gently, Jesus disengaged Himself from her and said, "Do not cling to Me, for I have not yet ascended to My Father . . ."

You see, Mary would have held on to Him forever just like Shulamite who said, "When I found the one I love, I held him and would not let him go."

Do you ever feel like that toward the Lord? Do the waves of emotion ever rise to overflowing in your soul so that you would cling to Him and hold Him forever to your heart? Shulamite brought her beloved to her mother's house. She wanted her family to know the One she loves.

Oh, there is a lesson there for us. Do we share Christ with others? Do we tell others about the One whom we love?

But there is another point in the verse—Not until we know the Lord intimately will we ever know or understand what true worship and blissful communion really are.

We must search the Scriptures, pray, seek His face with all our heart, and bring Him into our homes. Only those who have experienced Christ themselves are likely to direct others to Him.

Shulamite had a single-minded devotion to her beloved. Her love was so deep that it was stronger than death. She risked her life to find the one whom she loved.

Power of Love (8:6–7)

The power of love overwhelmed Shulamite and Solomon. Love is life itself; it is, if you will, eternity. Love is one of the two forces which no man can escape (the other is death, unless the rapture takes place) for love is as strong as death.

Listen, he who loves is dead to the world. You who love God in Christ are dead to the world and alive unto Christ. Paul said, "But God, who is rich in mercy, because of His great love with which He loved us, even when we were dead in trespasses, made us alive together with Christ" (Eph. 2:4–5).

DEATH IS THE ENEMY—LOVE IS THE VICTORY.

Paul said, "O death, where is your sting? . . . The sting of death is sin . . . But thanks be to God, who gives us the victory through our Lord Jesus Christ" (1 Cor. 15:55–57). This reminds us of God's passionate love for His people and His people for Him. God desires an intimate relationship with His people.

For Married Couples

For those of you who are married, keep intimacy alive.

1. God said intimacy in marriage is "Very Good" (Gen. 1:28, 31).

2. God designed marital intimacy to be completely without shame, filth, or ugliness (Heb. 13:4).

3. God designed intimacy for pleasure (Prov. 5:15–19; Song 5:10–16; 7:1–9).

4. God designed sexual intimacy for marriage (1 Cor. 7:1–2).

   If you are single, do not live as though you were married, and if you are married, do not live as though you were single. Sexual intimacy belongs only to a husband and his wife.

5. Marital intimacy is not an expression of selfish desire (1 Cor. 7:3–4).

   The pleasure and delight of each spouse does not come by fulfilling his or her own desires, but in satisfying the desires of the other person.

6. Marital intimacy is not to be set aside or postponed, except on very rare occasions (1 Cor. 7:5).

Don't let the fire die. If it is dying, refuel it. Cultivate it. Restart it. Don't wait; start at once to rekindle the fire and passion of love.

Like Shulamite, "I will seek the one I love, and when I found the one I love, I held him and would not let him go."

To All Christians:

1. Do you possess Shulamite's intensity of love for her beloved? Are you driven to seek Christ at all costs? If not, you will never know the joy and fulfillment of intimacy with God.

2. Do you perceive Christ's love for us? This love that was strong as death . . . He humbled Himself and became obedient to the point of death, even the death of the cross. (Phil. 2:8)

3. Do you plan to change your lifestyle in order to develop an intimate relationship with your beloved Christ?

4. If so, then pray and renew your vows; renew your commitment to Him.

7

Splendor

Song of Songs 3:6–11

AT THE BEGINNING OF the third poem, we have a reflection on the pomp and splendor of the wedding ceremony of Shulamite and King Solomon. The splendor of matrimony is revealed in the magnificent processional first observed at a distance.

It was awesome and mysterious, and when viewed close at hand, it was overpoweringly impressive in the majesty of its military procession and the exquisite details of every little thing. The entire scene embodies all the elements of royalty that ought to be accorded to a wedding and the couple at its center.

The seriousness and joy of the occasion warrant such careful attention. The transaction to be witnessed is of ultimate significance to the partners, their families, and the communities in which they live, and to the Lord, who, as our wedding ceremonies remind us, ordained marriage as the key social institution and is witness to and participant in each instance of it.

JEWISH WEDDING

The Jewish wedding ceremony is a beautiful event. It would take a complete chapter to cover all the logistics and explain the meaning behind each beautiful factor. However, I will give you a brief synopsis of the ceremonies:

1. *The Betrothal*

    This is the time when the arrangement for the marriage is contracted. The *Mohar* or dowry is given for the bride.

2. *The Procession*

    This is when the groom goes to the house in the middle of the night to steal the bride away. The groom is accompanied by a procession of groomsmen, and the best man shouts, "The Bridegroom is coming."

3. *The Wedding Ceremony*

    This is where the two are recognized as husband and wife in a legal sense.

    Notice the crown in Song of Songs 3:11. This crown is not the royal crown of Solomon's kingship, but a wedding crown. The custom of the ancient world was to crown the groom with a crown on his wedding day because the groom was considered a king that day. Hence Solomon's crown here is not the royal crown, but the wedding crown especially made for this occasion by his mother, Bathsheba.

    This crown or wreath bestowed by his mother (1 Kings 1:11) symbolizes a joyful celebration, like a wedding, not political and spiritual authority, which would have been bestowed by the chief priest (2 Kings 11:1–20), and required an armed military escort, as here in SOS 3.

    The practice of the wedding crown was discontinued with the destruction of Jerusalem in 70 AD. Today a wine glass is broken during a Jewish wedding ceremony to symbolize Jerusalem's destruction, for even on the occasion of a Jew's happiest day, the wedding day, Jerusalem must be remembered.

4. *The Wedding Feast or Banquet*

The feast or banquet follows the wedding ceremony. At this time the bride and groom anticipate the next event.

5. *The Wedding Night*

The couple becomes one in the flesh through their first sexual union. In fact, according to John 3:29, the groom then announces the consummation to the best man standing outside their door. The best man relays the announcement to the guests and families, and they celebrate for seven days—called "The 7 Days of Huppah." After seven days of embracing in passionate lovemaking, the bride and groom come out of their bridal chamber and, finding the guests still present, continue with more celebration, dancing, and festivities.

FEELINGS

All throughout the Song of Songs, we find Shulamite's admiration for her beloved Solomon and his ample and uninterrupted opportunity to display his feelings toward her. He boldly describes her beauty and worth publicly. He articulates his reverence of her. These are necessary components if the act of marriage is to have its proper meaning.

Nothing less than wholehearted esteem, especially on the part of us males who can be plagued by insecure arrogance and fickle wanderlust. Gentlemen, build a solid foundation of wholehearted esteem—love your wife, cherish her, and shout it from the mountain tops. Shout it to the world that she is the queen of your heart. That she is the most beautiful woman in the world. Let her know and let the world know that you love this woman.

Here comes the magnificent processional; first we see it from a distance, then close up.

Verse 6

"Who is this coming out of the wilderness?" This reminds us of Jesus triumphantly entering Jerusalem where the streets of the city are lined with a cheering, admiring throng. Unlike Solomon, the Greater Solomon, Christ rode into Jerusalem on an ass's colt.

The "pillars of smoke, perfumed with myrrh and frankincense, with all the merchant's fragrant powders," reminds us of Christ's birth. The pillar of smoke was actually incense or frankincense, and then there was myrrh. Gold, frankincense, and myrrh were brought to the infant Christ by the wise men.

Verses 7–8

The quiet, intimate scene of the beloved and the lover in her mother's bedroom in the last poem is eclipsed by the dazzle and decorum of a vast processional.

A practical lesson is found here in verses seven and eight and is valid today for a would-be husband. He should give proper thought and planning in protecting his bride and providing security for her. Another note regarding these soldiers: They were not only for the protection and security of Solomon's bride, but they may have been, in Solomon's case, a deterrent for possible assassination.

Erotic Romance (Verses 9–10)

The couch is a sedan chair made of the best wood from Lebanon. It is a portable lounging bed. The beauty of this portable bed is described in verses nine and ten. The silver, gold, and purple speak of opulent beauty.

"He made" emphasizes the fact that Solomon ordered the couch, as he had done for the interiors of the temple and his own palace.

"Its interior paved with love" means fitted out with love or lovemaking. It may hint that the couch was set up as the site of the nuptial embrace and given special tender touches by the daughters of Jerusalem. Simply, the interior décor of the couch may have been adorned with carved inlays of erotic scenes, such as was common in that part of the ancient world.

Verse 11

Eyes Only

I want you to notice something else. Jump down to verse 11.

Notice the exclusiveness of the relationship. Exclusiveness is a crucial strand in a marriage. The woman has eyes only for her Solomon despite the possible distraction of sixty hand-picked warriors.

The man's heart beats for her alone (look at 4:9–10 and 4:16 for a moment). He ties her as close to him as the nearest blood relative, a sister. He treasures the uniqueness of their bond—she is accessible to no one else; she is a garden which only his key can unlock.

4:11–12

She puts it simply and best . . .

4:16

"Forsaking all others, will you keep yourself only unto her / only unto him?"

"I do!"

This is the central question of the wedding ceremony. It is to be asked and answered at the beginning of the union and every day thereafter. Answering it with a fervent "yes" will not guarantee untarnished happiness. But it will provide the only context within which true happiness becomes a possibility.

LOOKING FOR THE BRIDE

Song of Songs 3:6–11 reminds me of something greater. One day all the simple folk of the countryside will be astir and filled with great interest and wonder as they behold a grand procession winding its way along the highway up from the glorious City of God. The outriders and trumpeters on prancing chargers herald the approach of a royal processional.

In the Hebrew, the question in verse 6 is "who is she that comes out of the wilderness?" Who is the honored bride called to share the love of the King?

Evidently at first, the people look in vain for a sight of her. Everything proclaims a nuptial parade, but no bride is really seen. In verse 11, however, the bridegroom is clearly visible. It is the son of David himself. This portrays the glorious reality which the bride of the Lamb shall soon know when the Shepherd-king comes to claim His own.

Book of Revelation

In Revelation 4 we find the rapture taking place where the Bridegroom comes for His bride, the Church. The first thing we see is a glorious throne and "One sat on the throne. And He who sat there was like a jasper and a sardius stone in appearance" (speaking of His first and second coming; 4:2–3). This One who sat on the throne was the "Lord God Almighty, who was and is and is to come" (Rev. 4:8).

In chapter 4 we learn that we will receive crowns at the judgment seat of Christ and that we will cast our crowns before the throne saying, "You are worthy, O Lord, to receive glory and honor and power; for You created all things, and by Your will they exist and were created" (4:11).

In chapter 5 we find the Lamb, the Lion of Judah, the root of David is worthy to open the scroll of judgments—and the tribulation begins.

By the time we get to Revelation 19, we find the marriage celebration, the marriage supper of the Lamb, where the bride, the Church, is beautifully arrayed in white before the King of Kings. And heaven rejoices, praises, and worships God, who sat on the throne, saying "Amen! Alleluia, praise be to our God Alleluia for the Lord God omnipotent reigns." Let us be glad and rejoice and give Him glory for the marriage of the Lamb has come and his wife has made herself ready.

Then we see the heavens roll back as a scroll and all of heaven's glory is revealed as Christ, the Son of David, the faithful and true, His eyes like a flame of fire, and His name is called the Word of God.

And the bride and all the host of heaven will be with Him. And the world will behold this awesome processional of power and praise as the potentate of the universe takes His creation all back.

Just like in Solomon's procession, the world will try to see the bride, but she is protected by the royal guard of Christ and the King of the Universe. King Jesus is seen with the crowns of glory and power and strength upon His head. And all the armies of hell cannot prevail against the Bridegroom and His bride. And the bride, the Church, inherits all that belongs to the King, her Bridegroom.

"Now I saw a new heaven and a new earth . . . Then I, John, saw the holy city, New Jerusalem, coming down out of heaven from God . . . 'There shall be no more death, nor sorrow, nor crying. There shall be no more pain'" (Rev. 21:1–4). It is also interesting that John said, "There shall be no night there" (Rev. 21:25). There will be no night in the eternal, no fear of night.

Terror

Notice Shulamite mentions "night" in Song of Songs 3:8. "Night" has a demonic connotation because some Jewish traditions reveal a deep-seated dread or fear of demonic disruptions of the wedding night. Since we live in the era of electricity, it makes it hard for us to grasp the intensity with which the ancients feared the night.

More than likely, the terror or "fear in the night" had to do with vandalism or, in Solomon's case, assassination. The sixty valiant men mentioned were the armed guard of "the best of the best" troops that escorted the wedding procession and protected it.

Considering Jewish tradition, it's no wonder one of John's bright revelations about the life to come promises that there shall be no night.

APPLICATION

How can we apply this chapter of Scripture? Peter gives us some insight in 1 Peter 3:1–9.

For Wives:

1. Action or Behavior (vv. 1–2). Let your godly behavior speak on your behalf. Quiet submission will speak louder to your husband than anything else.

2. Be Reversible (beautiful inside and outside) (vv. 3). Peter is not saying to "ignore the way you look!" He is telling wives not to spend all their time making the outside look good when the inside is in a pitiful and disarrayed state. Wives should have character as well as beauty.

3. Be careful of Attitude (vv. 4). "Gentle" has the idea of genuine humility. "Quiet" indicates tranquility. These speak of strong character and self-control. She displays a quiet elegance and dignity; she is not churning within or contentious without.

4. Be careful of response (vv. 5–6). "Obey" means to pay close attention to or attend to the needs of someone. Sarah took time to learn what Abraham's needs were; she focused the bulk of her energy on meeting his needs.

   The text implies the command to "do what is right without being frightened by any fear."

For Husbands:

1. Dwell with your wife (v. 7). This is not just simply eating, sleeping, or occupying the same house. The thought is "being closely aligned or at home with another" or, simply, promoting and maintaining domestic harmony—living side-by-side, sharing moment-by-moment, together "for richer, for poorer; in sickness and in health; 'til death do you part."

2. Understand your wife (v. 7). This does not mean to live with your wife in an understanding way. This means study her, learn about her, and listen to what she says. Be sensitive to her involvements, cares, and concerns. Seek to understand the pressures in her life. Encourage her to share her fears, secrets, thoughts, and dreams with you.

3. Honor your wife (v. 7). The idea is that a husband considers his wife a valuable being, a precious treasure, worthy of high esteem. In fact, the word rendered *honor* here has been translated as "precious" in 1 Peter 1:19 referring to the worth of the blood of Christ. Honor (Gr. *Time*—tee may')—Precious (Gr. *Timios*—tim' ee—os from Time)

   "To honor" means action. Does your wife know you honor her? Have you told her? Do you demonstrate it to her? If not, start now. Could it be that your prayers have fallen on deaf ears because you do not honor your wife?

For All Christians: Inherit A Blessing (vv. 8–9)

We as believers are called to be of "one mind." This involves having the mind of Christ or becoming intimate with Him, like Shulamite and Solomon.

Paul said, "Let this mind be in you which was also in Christ Jesus . . ." (Phil. 2:5). "That I may know Him and the power of His resurrection, and the fellowship of His sufferings, being conformed to His death" (Phil. 3:10).

1. Have compassion

2. Love as brothers

3. Be tenderhearted

4. Don't get even—give blessing

Do these things knowing that our Lord is to return and receive us to Himself. One day, in great pomp and procession, the King and His bride will return and take their proper place in the kingdom (2 Peter 3:14–18).

8

Solomon: Poet

Song of Songs 4:1–7, Part 1

SONG OF SONGS 4:1–15 is the longest of Solomon's poems.

This poem comes on the heels of Shulamite searching with passion for her beloved in the dark of night. She awoke and did not find him at her side, so she searched for him in the streets of the city. She found him, or rather he found her, and the embrace was sweet because she was now with the one she loved. After finding him, she reflected on her wedding day, the processional, and all the splendor of that celebration. Oh, how she described that wedding day with great pomp and majesty. She even described Solomon's couch, their nuptial lounge bed.

Solomon now responds to her also remembering their wedding night. His words praise his bride's beauty. Three times he tells her she is beautiful.

Verse 1 & 7

"You are fair" means you are beautiful. Solomon is tenderly wooing her and expresses his love for his bride as he approaches her. He praises her for her beauty and mentions parts of her body. He begins with her eyes and then describes the intimate parts of her body and declares that her body has no flaw.

Verse 1

"Dove's Eyes behind Your Veil"

It was customary for the bride to be veiled on the wedding night; she would then remove the veil in the wedding chamber. This is why Rebekah immediately veiled herself when she learned the identity of Isaac, her husband-to-be in Genesis 24. This also explains why Laban was able to deceive Jacob with Leah on their wedding night (Gen. 29).

Solomon is saying Shulamite's eyes are gentle and communicate tenderness, like the cooing of doves. Her eyes are tranquil and reflect character, as the eyes are the windows of the soul. He is praising her calm and innocent character. Her eyes gleamed through the veil.

"Your Hair like a Flock of Goats"

To us in the West, this comparison seems a little silly and meaningless. However, it implies vitality and grace. Goats in Israel are mostly black. Seen from a distance, the dark hair of Israeli goats is beautiful in the sunset as flocks descend from the mountains. The slopes of Mount Gilead, rising from the Jordan Valley, are very bare and appear to be a brown-bronze color. (Mount Gilead is a mountain range east of the Jordan River in Gilead, known for its fertile pastures and many flocks (Mic. 7:14).) The goats' descent often presents a lovely view of an otherwise boring scene.

Shulamite's dark hair has the same beautiful quality and conveys the message that she is full of life and that there is nothing clumsy about her. Her hair is described as a flock of black goats seemingly dangling on a steep mountainside slope giving the appearance of hanging down on the sides of the cliffs. This is how the locks of Shulamite's hair appear to Solomon as they hang over her shoulders.

Understand what Solomon is doing here. He eloquently describes her head and upper torso with the same intimacy of detail and flair for artistry as an impressionistic sculptor molding a bust of his model. Her hair falls in undulating waves over her ears, neck, and shoulders with the quiet grace of a flock seen from a distance, seemingly caressing a hillside with gentle movement.

Solomon is very smooth here.

Verse 2

"Teeth like a Flock of Shorn Sheep"

Israel's sheep are primarily white. What Solomon is saying here is that her teeth are as smooth as shorn sheep after they have been washed. "Twins . . . none is barren" refers to a mother sheep which has not lost any of her young. This means Shulamite has all her teeth and also speaks of youth and purity. Understand that having all her teeth was quite an achievement indeed, considering the absence of dentistry and the meager knowledge of oral hygiene.

Verse 3

"Lips like a Strand of Scarlet, and Your Mouth Is Lovely"

Her lips are a scarlet crimson red surrounding a beautiful mouth. "The strand of scarlet" literally means "thread" referring to the perfect outline and delicately formed shape of her lips. This scarlet thread also reminds us of Rahab's scarlet rope in Josh. 2:18.

Her teeth and lips made her mouth beautiful. The word *mouth* also refers to her speech or speaking. Her speech or the sound of her voice is lovely to him.

"Temples . . . like Pomegranate . . ."

This phrase speaks of a rosy glow. Perhaps she is blushed with anticipation. Her face, her temples, and her neck, mouth, and eyes are desirable to kiss.

Verse 4

*"Neck like the Tower of David . . .
on Which Hang a Thousand Bucklers"*

Bucklers or shields were often hung on tower walls (Ezek. 27:11; 1 Macc. 4:57 (Apocrypha)). Solomon made five hundred golden shields, and they were put into the house of the Forest of Lebanon, according to 1 Kings 10:16–17. These served as the royal armory (Isa. 22:8), and some believe this was also known as the Tower of David.

Solomon is implying strength, erectness, and perhaps even aloofness, meaning her head will not easily be turned by the blandishments of other men. The portrait of strong beauty is embellished by the comparison of her tiered or layered necklaces to small round shields as mentioned a moment ago. Simply, Solomon feels that great dignity and strength are present in her beauty.

Verse 5

Upper Torso

He is comparing her upper torso with the softness of fawns. Looking on the soft coat of a little fawn makes a person want to stroke it. Solomon wanted his love to know that her soft and gentle beauty had kindled his desire for her, and he wished to express that desire with his embrace and caresses.

Verse 6

Here Solomon wants this night to last forever. The first two lines are identical to those of 2:17, and the deer-language in 4:6 helps to tie Poem 3 to Poem 2.

"The mountain of myrrh and hill of frankincense" echo what was stated in verse 5 describing the upper torso of his precious Shulamite. It also refers to what is known in other literature as the mount of Venus. Basically, Solomon's passion is inflamed with love and desire.

Verse 7

Cultural Standard

After describing the seven-fold beauty of his love—her eyes, hair, teeth, mouth, temples, neck, and breasts—Solomon concludes that all of her, every part of her, shares the beauty. He is totally satisfied with his bride. He is telling her that she is altogether beautiful and there is no flaw in her.

The purpose of this descriptive song is not evaluation, as though the lover were judging a beauty contest, but rather a public celebration of her worth to him and his consequent commitment to her. By carefully detailing that worth in images attractive to the ancient, Middle Eastern eye, he is underscoring how much he loves her, how deeply he wants her, and how firmly he intends to stay with her.

Do you remember how she described herself as simply common in chapters one and two? She felt that she did not meet the objective standards of beauty in her society. She was not as beautiful as the royal ladies of Solomon's court. Let me tell you something, very few people in any age meet their own particular culture's standard of beauty. A woman is beautiful in the eyes of her lover simply because he loves her. Every husband who genuinely loves his wife can say "To me you are beautiful, and there is no flaw in you."

You see, what she may have looked like to others is irrelevant. Her beauty is in the eye and heart of the one who beholds her. By this song of description, he singles her out, praises her, and pledges himself to her until death do them part. He is not comparing her to other women, but excluding all other women when he sings this song.

Gentlemen, look your dear wife in her eyes and say, "You are beautiful. There is no flaw in you. I am committed to you for forever."

If You Are Married:

1 Corinthians 7:3–4

1. Being committed to one's mate is not a matter of demanding rights but releasing rights.
2. There is no place for selfishness in a marriage.
3. We need to surrender ourselves to one another.
4. "Forsaking all others" involves making the choice to give up some choices.

Our culture values choice, or rather, having choices. "Keep all your options open; don't give up anything," people say. To them, it's like a recent ad says, "Four books, four bucks, and absolutely, positively, no commitment!" *You get, and you don't have to give up a thing.* Perfect . . . The ad is perfect for a book club. That's the kind I might sign up for. The problem comes when you expect major commitments in life, such as marriage, to come with the same promise. You get, and you don't have to give up a thing—that is a lie.

1. Commitment in marriage (forsaking all others) opens the door to the deeper meanings in life.
2. When people are more dedicated in marriage, they have more self-disclosure in their relationships.

3. When such a commitment exists, each will feel little risk in sharing deeply with the other. There is commitment and support (you can be counted on), and you are best friends because your commitment and dedication fosters trust. Far from limiting a couple, commitment is freeing.

4. This kind of commitment in action forms the basis of many years together as friends.

5. Hence, commitment in marriage—really sticking with full dedication—opens up the fuller depths of openness . . . naked and unashamed.

6. Commitment and dedication in marriage is like sanctification, consecration, and holiness. The concept is something being "pure and devoted," "separate," or "set apart" for a particular use or purpose, particularly for the purposes of God.

Practical Ways to Help Your Commitment and Dedication:

1. Make regular time to take a walk together, hold hands, and talk about interesting things (not all the problems of life). You have set apart a moment of connection together as friends.

2. When you make it a point to be home at dinnertime (or another special time) so that the family can have time together, you have set apart a special moment.

3. When you schedule a date to have some fun, you have set apart time.

4. When you make time in your schedules to work on problems and issues together, you have set apart some moments for keeping your marriage on track.

5. A person needs to hear "I love you" or to be hugged six times a day to remain emotionally healthy.

6. Don't forget to dance. (If you don't dance, turn on music, turn the lights down low, and simply hold each other).

For All Christians

1 Corinthians 6:19–20—Commitment glorifies God

Paul reminds us of two truths: First, we are not our own but have been purchased with Christ's blood on the cross. Second, the Christian's ultimate goal in life is not to be happy, but to glorify God.

As we glorify Him:

1. Seek to do His will rather than our own.

2. He will see to it that our essential needs are either met or that our need for them will diminish.

3. Happiness may come at times when we are doing His will, but that is not what is most important.

4. Glorifying God is our all-encompassing goal.

5. Glorifying God involves commitment, and unswerving dedication to Him.

6. Like Solomon in the Song of Songs, Christ is completely committed to you. He will never leave you or forsake you (Heb. 13:5).

7. God sees you, His children, His bride, as "beautiful . . . with no flaw."

Paul said it this way,

> Therefore, just as the church is subject to Christ, so let the wives be to their own husbands in everything. Husbands, love your wives, just as Christ also loved the church and gave Himself for her, that He might sanctify and cleanse her with the washing of water by the word, that He might present her to Himself a glorious church, not having spot or wrinkle or any such thing, but that she should be holy and without blemish (Eph. 5:24–27).

Ladies and Gentlemen: These verses speak of our Lord's commitment and dedication to us, the example husbands and wives should emulate, and the obedience of all believers to follow in the footsteps of Christ in total commitment and dedication to Him and His cause.

9

Greater Love
Song of Songs 4:1–7, Part 2

IT IS NOT STRANGE that when we think of our Lord Jesus Christ, our heavenly Bridegroom, that our souls are moved to their deepest depths. But it is hard for us to realize that He has a greater love for us than we could ever possibly have for Him.

Here in this fourth chapter of Song of Songs, we hear the bridegroom expressing to his love the feelings of his heart toward her. Prophetically, we may think of the bride as Israel, and Jehovah rejoicing over her in that coming day. Individually, we may think of the bride as representing any saved soul and the Lord expressing His delight in the one He has redeemed to Himself by His precious blood. Or the bride could represent the Church in general, which Christ loved and for which He gave Himself.

In this section of verses, Solomon once more tells his beloved Shulamite how greatly he loves her and assures her that, when the time is ripe, he will be ready to come and carry her away from all the dangers and temptations. He describes her beauties—these are the beauties of the church and the precious redeemed souls consisting in the beauty of holiness.

Those that honor Christ, He will honor—"For those who honor Me I will honor . . ." (1 Sam. 2:30). O beloved, the Lord looks upon His Church and sees us without spot or blemish (Eph. 5:27).

YOU ARE FAIR, MY LOVE!
BEHOLD, YOU ARE FAIR!

Christ sees in us something we cannot see in ourselves. Solomon expresses his desire for Shulamite and describes her beauty. Shulamite said, "O my Shepherd, My King, I am dark . . .like the tents of Kedar, like the curtains of Solomon." But he says as he looks at her through love's eyes, "You are beautiful, my love" (Song of Songs 1).

Does this not remind us of the wondrous thing that our Savior has done for every one of us who have been redeemed by the precious blood of Christ? We would never have been saved at all if we had not realized in some measure our own wickedness, our own sinfulness, our own unlovely character. Because of this realization, we fled to Him for refuge and confessed that we were anything but fair, anything but beautiful.

Like Job, we cried out and said, "I have heard of You by the hearing of the ear, but now my eye sees You. Therefore I abhor myself, and repent in dust and ashes" (Job 42:5–6). We knelt along with Isaiah and said, "I am a man of unclean lips, and I dwell in the midst of a people of unclean lips" (Isa. 6:5). We took part with Peter in saying, "Depart from me, for I am a sinful man, O Lord!" (Luke 5:8)

When we repented and acknowledged our sinfulness and our unloveliness, Christ looked at us in His grace and said, "You are forgiven and accepted in the Beloved; behold you are beautiful, my love."

Once it could be said of us, as Isaiah penned down, "From the sole of the foot even to the head, there is no soundness in it, but wounds and bruises and putrefying sores; they have not been closed or bound up, or soothed with ointment" (Isa. 1:6). But now His holy eyes cannot find one spot of sin, nor any sign of iniquity.

"Amazing grace, how sweet the sound, that saved a wretch like me." It is only God's matchless grace that has made us accepted in the Beloved.

Paul said, "And you He made alive, who were dead in trespasses and sins, in which you once walked according to the course of this world . . .But God, who is rich in mercy, because of His great love with which He loved us, even when we were dead in trespasses, made us alive together with Christ (by grace you have been saved), and raised us up together, and made us sit together in the heavenly places in Christ Jesus" (Eph. 2:1, 4).

Regarding the beauty of the Church, the images are certainly very bright, the shadows are very strong, and the comparisons acutely bold. A sevenfold description of the beauty of the Church is brought to our attention through Solomon's expression of praise, love, and adoration of Shulamite.

PERFECT

Seven is the number of perfection, for the Church is enriched with manifold graces by the seven spirits that are before the throne (Rev. 1:4; 1 Cor. 1:5, 7).

YOU HAVE DOVE'S EYES BEHIND YOUR VEIL

This means not only that we have eyes of beauty, but eyes quick to discern the precious and wonderful things that are hidden for us in His Holy Word. Those who go on to spiritual maturity are able to perceive the things of the Spirit.

You know the eyes tell the secrets of the heart. To know what another person is thinking we need only watch that person's face, particularly his eyes. The shifty eye reveals deceit, the glaring eye anger, the tear-filled eye sorrow, the dancing eye mischief, and the soulful eye love.

The dove is symbolic of the Holy Spirit. As Christ looks at His Church, as He looks at us, what catches and holds His eye is the joy of seeing the Holy Spirit indwelling the believer. How wonderful it would be if, every time the Lord Jesus looked at us, He could see that wonderful Holy Spirit of love, joy, peace, grace, truth, wisdom, faith, and power shining out of our eyes.

The dove's eyes are behind a veil, which speaks of a shade over them and implies, on one hand, that the eyes cannot fully see. As long as we are here in this world, we know only in part. On the other hand, this means that the people of the world cannot see or understand what a believer with spiritual perception sees. The world cannot understand spiritual things. This is why it is in vain to speak to the unsaved in a language that is simply babble to them. Spiritual things can only be understood by spiritual persons. Spiritual understanding and spiritual perceptions are hidden from the world. The world simply does not understand what Christians understand. This lack of understanding is why tension exists between those whose citizenship belongs to the world and those whose citizenship belongs to heaven.

YOUR HAIR IS LIKE A FLOCK OF GOATS, GOING DOWN FROM MOUNT GILEAD

Hair in Scripture reminds us of at least two things:

1. Special consecration and obedience, as in the case of the Nazarites.

   A Nazarite's hair was his symbol of consecration, which becomes his strength. This strength was easily seen by people because the long hair was an outward symbol of inner strength.

   As we are obedient to the Lord and as we consecrate ourselves to Him, the degree that we separate ourselves unto Him is the degree or measure of our strength before men. Separation unto God is the key to unlock spiritual strength. Our holiness unto God or our spiritual strength comes from the holiness of the heart.

2. The woman's hair that is the symbol of her glory and of the special majesty with which God has crowned her (1 Cor. 11:14–15).

Do you remember the woman of old who loved Jesus and knelt at His feet, washing them with her tears and wiping them with her hair? She was using that which spoke of her beauty and her glory to minister to Him, the loving, blessed Savior.

What the Lord Jesus wants to see in us is a display of the majesty He confers on each believer. We are betrothed to heaven's Beloved. He has bestowed upon us a majesty beyond that given to any other creature. Just as a woman's hair is her glory, we should display by our character, conduct, and conversation the majesty and glory which is ours. The woman's hair symbolically speaks of subjection and being obedient, like the woman who wiped the Lord's feet with her hair.

LIKE THE GOATS WHO FEAST ON THE HILLS OF GILEAD

When the Lord makes known His will, the obedient Christian bows to His authority, assured that there is a reason for it, though he does not always understand it. How our Beloved delights to behold His obedient, yielding, and yet, glorious and majestic people. He glories in their moral, spiritual, and glorious beauty.

YOUR TEETH ARE LIKE A FLOCK OF SHORN SHEEP WHICH HAVE COME UP FROM THE WASHING, EVERY ONE OF WHICH BEARS TWINS, AND NONE IS BARREN AMONG THEM

"Your teeth" in verse 2 speaks of feeding, chewing, chomping, gnawing, dining, devouring, and eating. An infant cannot chew food, so this verse is implying maturity and the ability to feed ourselves and to properly chew and digest our food. Mature believers, not baby Christians who can only handle milk, are represented by Shulamite.

I am afraid there are a number of toothless Christians today who say, "I do not know how other people read their Bibles and find such wonderful things, but I do not find much in mine." The trouble is these Christians have such poor teeth, and they do not chew their spiritual food properly. Until Christ gives you a new set of spiritual teeth, you had better use some second-hand ones.

Thank God for what others have found; read their books, and get something that way. By and by, if you will wait on Him, the Lord will give you a set of teeth so you will be able to enjoy the truth for yourself. Through meditation, we appropriate our daily provision. David said, "May my meditation be sweet to Him" (Ps. 104:34).

Your Teeth Are like a Flock of Shorn Sheep

You see, sheep graze on pasture and can distinguish what is good for them and what is not good. A mature believer can differentiate between what is Christ's and what is not. As teachers of the Word, we must chew the meat and give it to the babies, the infants in the church, so they can grow.

Notice the comparison of shorn sheep. In the Old Testament, wool indicates the carnal life and human zeal. The priests, when entering into the Holy Place, were forbidden to wear garments of wool. They were to use linen. Fine white linen is symbolic of the righteousness Christ imparted through the Holy Spirit.

The fact that Shulamite's teeth were like a flock of shorn sheep implies her strength and ability to apply, to understand, and to digest spiritual things. This was something that did not come from natural ability, but rather a spiritual reality, a spiritual ability.

Come up from the Washing, Every One of Which Bears Twins

"Come up from the washing" speaks of cleansing and sanctification, of being clean and thoroughly washed from all that is unsuitable so as to walk orderly in His ways.

Which bears twins speaks of orderliness and implies progressive strength and the ability to digest and discern.

Shulamite's teeth were perfect. There was nothing to mar her smile. Is there anything that mars our smile?

One of the great beauties of the believer should be his smile, a smile born of the joy that comes from within, expressed at all times and in all circumstances. Joy is much deeper than mere happiness. Happiness depends on what happens. Joy, on the other hand, is the fruit of the Spirit.

Do not grieve the Holy Spirit with known sin in your life. When our Bridegroom beholds us, let Him see the indwelling Spirit's overflowing joy.

YOUR LIPS ARE LIKE A STRAND OF SCARLET, AND YOUR MOUTH IS LOVELY

Just as the teeth are instruments for receiving and chewing food, so the lips are an expression of what we receive from Him. "Like a strand of scarlet" speaks of spiritual health. Red lips are a sign of health; the paleness of the lips is a sign of faintness or weakness. "Scarlet" speaks of redemption and reminds us of Rahab's scarlet thread in her window (Josh. 2:21). It also speaks of authority for our mouth reflects our motive and heart. The mouth, like the human eye, is an expressive part of the face. It can register hardness or tenderness, sorrow or pain, or surprise, humor, or horror.

Shulamite, the bride, loved to speak to her bridegroom. Her lips and mouth testified to that fact. The Christian loves to speak to Christ and of Christ, and our lips are like a thread of scarlet. We have been redeemed by the blood of the Lamb, and from our lips the Church, the Christian, loves to speak of Christ, and we exalt that blood by which we have been brought near to God. Every Christian gladly confesses that he owes everything for eternity to that precious atoning blood of the Lord Jesus Christ. We love to sing, speak, and think of the blood; always, everywhere, at all times, the believer delights to remember that he has been redeemed to God by the precious blood of Christ.

The scarlet thread runs all the way through the Scripture. *God said,*

> For the life of the flesh is in the blood, and I have given it to you upon the altar to make atonement for your souls; for it is the blood that makes an atonement for the soul (Lev. 17:11).

> When I see the blood, I will pass over you" (Ex. 12:13).

> We have been redeemed to God by the precious blood of Christ (Rev. 5:9).

> The blood of Jesus Christ [God's] Son cleanses us from all sin (1 John 1:7).

Where is all this world today? Can the Lord Jesus find words to fill His loving heart with joy, unless those words come from the lips of His own bride? The Word says, "with our tongue we will prevail; our lips are our own; who is lord over us?" (Ps. 12:4) Nobody else can speak the language of Zion; nobody else has a mouth capable of expressing the thoughts He wants to hear.

Our beloved Lord listens to the babble of noise that ascends on high from this earth in a thousand tongues. He is listening for those who speak His language, the language of heaven. He is listening for someone who will say from their heart:

> My Jesus I love thee, I know thou art mine,
> for thee all the follies of sin I resign

He is listening for you. Do not speak at random or uncontrolled. Speak with purity and holiness. Don't be satisfied with a namby-pamby, spineless, bloodless religion of today.

Tens of thousands of people say they are Christians and know nothing of trusting in the precious blood of the Lord Jesus alone for salvation. They know nothing of the cleansing value of the blood of Christ. Be sure you are trusting in His blood.

YOUR TEMPLES BEHIND YOUR VEIL ARE LIKE A PIECE OF POMEGRANATE

The temples indicate beauty or thought. Regarding thought: the bride loves to think of him and to meditate upon the treasures of his word. Isn't it true that lovers enjoy hearing each other's voices? Shulamite loved to hear the voice of her lover. The Christian loves to meditate and hear the voice of our heavenly Beloved through His Word. He delights in her as she delights in Him.

The pomegranate in biblical language points to fullness of life because of its many seeds, each of which is juicy, sweet, and red. This speaks of fruit in the life of a believer. Fruit comes from listening to His Word. Such fruit manifests the beauty of holiness hidden behind the veil, meaning that such spiritual qualities are hidden from the world because the world does not understand spiritual things.

Only the Lord sees the beauty of holiness, the beauty of fruit, the beauty of meditation. This beauty is only displayed before the Lord's eyes and in the community of believers.

YOUR NECK IS LIKE THE TOWER OF DAVID

The Tower of David was built to be a storehouse of weapons. The weapons show strength being within the tower. These weapons were not for offense, but for defense. The idea conveyed by this comparison is that Shulamite was watchful.

David was "a man after [God's] own heart, who [did] all God's will" (Acts 13:22). And just like David, Shulamite was obedient and submissive. She fully surrendered to the Lord, and she was steadfast and immovable, like a tower, doing the will of God. She was alert and on her defense with a sufficiency in inward weapons against any inroad by the enemy.

The bride can stand up straight and boldly look the world in the face, assured of the love and protection of her matchless bridegroom: And so we are called upon to "be strong in the Lord and in the power of his might" (Eph. 6:10).

YOUR TWO BREASTS ARE LIKE TWO FAWNS, TWINS OF A GAZELLE, WHICH FEED AMONG THE LILIES

... shape, carefully veiled behind the long ... the flowing contours of her veil. He sees ... . Full development does not come all at ... ng out the beauty of the flower, to grow a ... row into a mature young woman.

... at God is never in a hurry whether it be ... ms like such a long time since the Lord ... y. It seems like such a long time since the ... into this world. The Holy Spirit has been ... nd years patiently bringing the Church

... es of God in the Church have been al-... seems to be very slow pace. How much ... You return? One day the Church will be ... e last soul will enter the Body of Christ. ... day on Earth for the Church. Soon, the ... glory. Even so come, Lord Jesus.

We feed kids!

www.israeltodayministries.org

P.O. Box 150288
Arlington, Texas 76015
Facebook.com/IsraelTodayMinistries
itmdrjeff@gmail.com

Jeffrey D Johnson, President
Humanitarian, Educator, Author

Israel Today Ministries

10

Intimacy: Par Excellence
Song of Songs 4:8—5:1

As SHULAMITE AND SOLOMON reflect on their wedding night in this third poem of the Song, we now come to a most intimate description of their honeymoon.

Solomon up to now has praised Shulamite for the outward beauties which he saw. He described her eyes, hair, teeth, lips, temples, neck, and breasts, but now he begins to extol the beauties of her love by what he experiences in their first intimate physical union on their wedding night.

Verse 8

Be Alone

The commitment implied in the description song in verses 1–7 is made explicit here in verse 8 by its unmistakable words of invitation. By his addressing her as "my spouse," the bond is sealed. The Hebrew word for *spouse* suggests permanent incorporation of the woman into the man's family and can be translated either as bride, which applies to verse 8, or as daughter-in-law, such as in Ruth's case. Since the word *spouse* is used only in Poem 3 of the Song, it adds weight to the argument that this section of the book describes the actual wedding events.

The mountains mentioned here are literal mountains. The mountain range of Hermon is located in the northern part of Israel and northwest of Damascus. This reference is probably describing the southern part of the Hermon which can be seen from the Galilee where Shulamite grew up. Hermon's snowy peaks feed the Jordan River, which feeds the Sea of Galilee and flows into the Dead Sea.

The references to "lions" and "leopards" denote that Solomon was desirous to take Shulamite to the mountains on their honeymoon to be alone in a remote and peaceful place and perhaps with some animal-watching thrown in. Lions and leopards were a regular part of Israel's ecology well into the Christian era. Today, these animals are once again being seen in this area. The beasts may add to the erotic mood since Canaanite mythology records accounts of the goddess of love likened to a lion.

Simply, Solomon is filled with desire to be alone with his bride and asked his precious Shulamite to travel with him in order to view some erotic and exotic sights.

Verse 9

"You have ravished my heart." Solomon uses this phrase twice for emphasis. This describes Solomon's ecstasy as the very look of Shulamite begins to ravish Solomon toward intimate arousal.

When Solomon uses the word *sister* here, this conveys no intimation of incest. In Middle Eastern thought, the view of family ties bind together all family members into one personality. It is a term of exquisite endearment that promises the beloved a place in her husband's life as close as that of a blood relative. The two view themselves virtually as one person.

The reference to "eyes" has always played a featured role in interpersonal communication. The bride's "come hither" gaze, though just a brief glance, just one look, has added to her lover's stimulation.

"Link of your necklace" is simply a reference to her garments. Solomon now begins to initiate foreplay and further describes the features of his bride.

Verses 10–11

Touching

At verse 10 talk has led to touch. The caressing that the beloved yearned for has begun.

"Your love" means "your acts of loving" which are being extolled and experienced simultaneously. "Wine" is a figure of love's exhilaration. "Scent of your perfumes" captures the natural fragrance of her body aglow with her response to his touch and with her anticipation of their total union. "Than all spices" is Solomon saying that Shulamite's body alone outdoes all the fragrances he mentions. Solomon has praised her for her outward beauties, but now he will extol the beauties of her love according to what he experiences in their first intimate union as one flesh.

Verse 11

Kissing

Here we find the kissing that arouses them both. Do you remember Shulamite's initial wish in Song of Songs 1:2—"Let him kiss me with the kisses of his mouth"? In Song of Songs 4:3, Solomon praises how her lips and mouth look, and here in 4:11, he lauds their taste—they are like "honeycomb; honey and milk . . ." A favorite biblical metaphor of sweetness is honey and milk whose combination made the promised land of Canaan attractive to Israel's wilderness wanderers.

"Under your tongue" points to the depth and fullness of the kissing. Solomon, like any wise lover, has not rushed the pace. It is union and communion, not relief or release that he seeks. He gives praise and pleasure at each stage.

Verses 12–15

Rightful Owner

Solomon now turns to contemplate the final step, his entry into the inmost chamber of her personhood, the most precious expression of her femininity, which he describes in a cluster of terms that signal beauty, privacy, refreshment, and exclusiveness. In his beautiful description of the lower torso of his beloved Shulamite, we find sensual images of their experience together as husband and wife.

Shulamite's chamber of the most precious expression of femininity is described in terms of a garden, which was not unusual in the ancient world. The "garden enclosed" implies protection from the ravages of marauders and the prying eyes of the curious, open only to him who has its key. "A spring shut up" means locked or fastened with its precious liquid reserved for private use. Her husband has rightful access. "A fountain sealed" is a phrase synonymous with the preceding; it implies one that is shut up against all impurities and means no one else has ever had her. She was kept from all the impurities of fornication or, in other words, Shulamite is a virgin.

Solomon, her husband, the rightful owner, the one who owns the key, now desires sexual satisfaction with her and only by her will he be satisfied.

"Your plants" (v. 13) in Hebrew may mean tunnel, canal, or watercourse or also branches or limbs and could refer to her legs or the obvious lower portion of her body being described in the previous verse.

In these verses, we have a summary of the finest fragrances that made their bridal chamber delightful.

The word *orchard* can also be translated "paradise."

"A fountain of gardens, a well of living waters" means running waters that are artesian, fed by an inexhaustible underground supply. "Streams from Lebanon" shows a picture of bounty. The snow packs on the high mountains guarantee a spate of water unmatched in Israel's seasonal streams that fill and empty according to the rhythms of the rainfall.

These verses express that foreplay has reached a stage of excitement that has fueled great passion and anticipation of the ultimate union between husband and wife which we find in verse 16.

Verse 16

To Enter

"Awake" has the same meaning as "stir up." "Come" literally means to enter, come in, or to penetrate. The west wind brings rain; the east wind is hot and withering. But the "north wind" clears the air with cool breezes, and the "south" wind brings warmth. Thus, the north and south winds promote growth if they come and interchange at proper times. As a result, the entire garden becomes a sea of incense and fragrance, and the garden itself blows out its odor with fragrant plants.

Shulamite is ready and now invites Solomon to enjoy the holy union that is ordained for husband and wife. Solomon waited until she was ready for him, and now she signals that she is ready. Solomon is invited to enjoy his garden, for they belong to each other.

Messiah

This is a beautiful section of the Song of Songs. It reminds us of Christ's love for His Church. These words are His words to His bride, His spouse, and are the expression of His affection to her. There is a marriage covenant between Christ and His Church, between Christ and every true believer. The Church is the bride of Christ (Rev. 21:9; Eph. 5:22–32; 2 Cor. 11:2).

The gracious call Solomon gives to Shulamite to come with Him reminds us that all who come to Christ by faith must go with Christ. We must go with Him in obedience and compliance to His call. Being joined to Him, we must walk with Him.

Solomon's desire for Shulamite to come to the high mountains to get away alone together reminds us of Christ's call to His bride to come away from the world below and join Him in the high places of intimate fellowship with Him.

This is a call to "come out from among them and be separated" (2 Cor. 6:17). He wants us to come out from under the dominion of temptation and the world's pressures, which are as lions and leopards, and to rest and fellowship with Him on top of the mountain.

Solomon would have paid a dowry or "mohar" for his beloved Shulamite. Christ has purchased you, the Church, with His own blood (Acts 20:28).

The garden is the church in which a beautiful fragrance of praise and adoration is offered to the Lord. As Shulamite invites Solomon to come to his garden, the true Christian invites Christ to take what is rightfully His. We say, "Lord, here is my life. Take it and do what you will. I am yours and you are mine. Take my life, and let it be consecrated completely to you. Take my life, and I will follow you forever, only all for you."

Verse 16

His Garden

Shulamite, responding to her beloved shepherd's words, opened herself completely to him, inviting him to take his rightful place. She yielded fully without reservation to him. This is what our Shepherd's words can do for us. If we are occupied with Him and His Word, then we will respond, opening our hearts, our lives, our trust, and our future to the One we love.

She said to him, "Let my beloved come to his garden." She says, in effect, "Ah! You have been telling me that I am a garden of delights, a pomegranate paradise, and a lovely park in a wilderness world. Well, beloved, I am all yours . . ."

Surely the heart's cry of the believer, overwhelmed with the love of the Savior, is "Come Lord Jesus! I am yours! Take me to yourself! Even so, come, Lord Jesus."

And what will our Beloved say to that? The next section of the Song tells us.

11

Honeymoon Over?

Song of Songs 5:1–9

Verse 1

HERE WE FIND THE consummation of the marriage. The union of two becoming one is a beautiful mystery that God ordained for husband and wife.

This is the picture of the union between Christ and the Church at the consummation of the age when the rapture takes place and the bride and the Bridegroom become one. "Oh, what a day that will be when my Jesus I shall see, I shall look upon His face the One who saved me by His grace. When He takes me by the hand and leads me to the promise land, what a day, glorious day that will be."

Verse 1b

The second part of verse 1 reminds us of the Jewish custom, "The 7 Days of Huppah" (mentioned in Chapter Seven). The bride's veil is removed, and all know and see the bride's face that is behind this mysterious head covering.

Verse 2

This is the beginning of the fourth poem in the Song of Songs. The wedding is over; the dust and clamor of the pomp and ceremony that dominated the third poem have settled. The text does not give us a hint as to the passing of time between the two poems. Whether it is days, weeks, or months, we don't know. What we do know is that passion still runs high, but the satisfaction of that passion may be delayed by the lovers' differences in schedule, energy, health, or personal circumstances.

In this poem, we find Shulamite is once again having a troubled dream. In her last dream, which came many times, the cause was a result of a very real and long winter's separation early in their relationship.

The dream in this poem occurs only once and portrays the realisms of married life with its rhythm of frustration and delight. The two partners are not always ready for lovemaking at the same time or one partner may not even be available when the other is eager. Such frustrations are painful and can stretch the covenant bond. This poem reminds us that a sense of humor can keep frustration from souring into bitterness.

"My heart is awake" suggests either a dream or the twilight zone between sleep and wakefulness when our imaginations play tricks on our understanding of reality.

"It is the voice of my beloved" implies that the lover's eagerness is highlighted in the lure of his voice.

"He knocks" means he is knocking in an urgent manner, almost beating or banging at the door.

He says, "Open for me." He is begging her, and his begging is emphasized by the quartet of endearing names—"my sister, my love, my dove, my perfect one". . .my little baby . . . hubba hubba hubba.

"My locks" refers to his curly hair. "Drops of the night" either references the dew of the evening meaning it was summer or springtime or references the fact that he is drenched with dew expressing the urgency of his desire.

His absence at bedtime may mean that he was working because of some agricultural task, such as tending to sick animals or helping ewes drop their lambs. His work kept him in the fields until early morning, and he was coming in from a hard night's work.

Verse 3

"Taken off my robe" refers to the ancient world custom of sleeping without garments. She was already in bed.

"I have washed my feet." In the Middle East, people wore sandals, and in the course of the day, the feet became soiled with the dust and dirt. So, prior to bedtime, the feet would be washed.

In other words, Shulamite's response is that she is lying in bed, her feet are already washed, her undergarment is off, and she is quite unwilling to get up. Getting up would mean that she would have to put on again that which had been taken off and her feet that had been washed would be soiled again.

Solomon has one thing on his mind, but Shulamite is exhausted . . . and says no. Keep in mind this is only a dream, but it is based on reality.

At this point, Shulamite gives Solomon faulty excuses and rejects his romantic overtures.

Verse 4

Breaking In

Solomon, so very anxious to be with his wife, stretches his hand through the latch of the door either to try to open it or as a plea to her to open the door. Regardless, Solomon's effort to have the door opened by putting his hand through the lattice window demonstrates his longing for Shulamite. His action gets her attention, and it stirs her heart.

"My heart yearned for him." She begins to respond to his longing for her. She is thoroughly alert now and was aroused to the point of churning, yearning for him, desiring him. So, Shulamite got up to open the door (v. 5).

Verse 5

"My hands dripped with myrrh" speaks of a custom where a lover places perfumed ointment or oil on the bolt of a girl's door when he comes and she is not there. Solomon brought costly myrrh as for a festival, for to be with Shulamite was to Solomon a feast indeed.

Some of the myrrh dropped off on the handle of the bolt of the door when Solomon stretched his hand through the lattice window. For all practical purposes, Shulamite may as well not have been home. Or the drop could have been from Shulamite who may have squeezed the "liquid" from the bag between her breasts (1:13). Either way it is possible. Another possibility is that the myrrh, such as in 4:6, had secreted a fragrant invitation to her husband for whose embraces she was totally prepared.

Nevertheless, when Shulamite opened the door, Solomon was gone.

Verse 6

"My heart (or soul) leaped up when he spoke" means she was deeply impressed or deeply moved. His voice had aroused her beyond control, and she was willing to take any risk, as we will find out, to be with him. She now understands that she did not respond properly to the deep impression of his loving words.

She quickly dresses and runs out to find him. As she seeks him, she fails to find him. When she calls for him, she hears no answer. "I sought him, but I could not find him; I called him, but he gave me no answer."

You see, Solomon completely *turned away* from Shulamite in utter disappointment over her failure to open up to him and because she gave such flimsy excuses.

Verse 7

Mistaken Identity

In the course of her wandering around the city, the night watchmen find her, and mistaking her for a prostitute, treat her roughly. In order to escape arrest, she struggles, leaves her upper garment, and manages to get away from them. (This reminds us of Joseph's similar experience in Genesis 39 with Potiphar's wife.)

The lewd acts of the watchmen—wounding her, bruising her, and taking her veil, which is a reference to her shawl and probably the only piece of clothing that she had quickly thrown over her head and upper body for cover from prying eyes—are recorded to intensify the picture of the woman's passion and her single-hearted desire to find her lover, her husband, even in circumstances that left her vulnerable to terror.

These so-called keepers of the walls became muggers, not protectors. The fact that she pauses, neither to give vent to her feelings of shame, nor to call for the watchmen's punishment, seems to pinpoint the sharpness of her focus. She wanted to find her husband, her lover, her protector.

Now Shulamite, in her dream, turns to the daughters of Jerusalem and implores their help.

Verse 8

She attempts to recruit the aid of the daughters of Jerusalem to help her find Solomon. The setting for this verse comes at the end of the dream sequence, if it is still in progress, or early the next morning when Shulamite recounts to them the whole story.

The intensity of passion is still the dominate theme; however, those passions failed to find fulfillment.

"Lovesick" here seems to describe frustration from sexual abstinence rather than exhaustion from intimate activity as in Song of Songs 2:5. Shulamite said to the daughters of Jerusalem, "If you find Solomon, tell Him I will respond to him. Tell Him that my attitude has changed."

Verse 9

Mocking

The daughters of Jerusalem are seemingly making light of the whole situation and trying to lighten the mood with their playful questions. The rapid switches in scene and tone are easily explained if the whole context is a dream because dreams do things like that.

Their fourfold use of "beloved" echoes Shulamite's favorite name for Solomon. They may be mimicking the frequency with which Shulamite used it because she used the term "beloved" five times in verses 2–8.

"O fairest among women" may be an effort to reassure Shulamite that no one so attractive will be neglected for long by her husband. But the phrase also has a poetic role: it serves as a suspense-building line that postpones the final, punch-like clause of the question. The repetition of the first two lines in lines four and five add to that effect.

"That you so charge us" takes us back to verse 8 and asks what is so all-consuming and excellent about your lover that you go to the extravagance of binding us by an oath to tell him how frantic your love is. Basically, the daughters of Jerusalem respond by asking what makes your husband so special that they should bother to help in the search.

What is so special about Solomon that Shulamite has given herself to him and has experienced great pain in the process? And what is so special about Solomon that she implores them to help her find him? She responds to those questions in the following verses.

However, before we find out what is so special about Solomon, let's look at the following—

If you are married, take heed to three things:

1. Maintain good communication: The most common cause of communication breakdown is that individuals dig in their heels and insist on their rights rather than trying to understand each other.

2. Thrive and grow sexually: Unhealthy marriages exhibit reduced frequency of physical contact and a lack of compassion in the midst of sexual contact.

3. Develop true spirituality: It is hard to destroy a relationship that is built by two people who love God and are committed to obeying His command to love each other, pray together, confess their needs, and exchange ideas, feelings, and thoughts regarding their spiritual walk.

This wonderful section in Song of Songs 5 reminds us of Christ, our Beloved, knocking on the door of our heart and how we give frivolous excuses to our Bridegroom. Christ calls to us to open to him, but we pretend we have no time, nor strength to open the door. We do not want to get out of our warm bed of complacency.

Just like Solomon put his hand through the door, attempting to open the lock, so it is with the Holy Spirit. The Holy Spirit longs to open our heart's door. And like Lydia of Acts 16, "the Lord opened her heart to heed the things spoken by Paul" (16:14), perhaps the Lord is speaking to your heart right now.

Just like Solomon left evidence that he had been there (Shulamite's "hands dripped with myrrh; [her] fingers with liquid myrrh" (Song of Songs 5:5)) so it is when Christ comes into your life in a powerful way. He leaves a blessed sweetness, and it will be obvious that you have been with Christ.

She did not open the door

O beloved, seek Him while He may be found. Don't let time slip away. Don't wait until it is too late.

Just as the daughters of Jerusalem acknowledged Shulamite's beauty, so it is at times with those outside the Church. They can see the beauty of the holiness of the Church, the beauty of the bride of

Christ; even though they may have little acquaintance with Christ, they can see that beauty in those that bear His image.

On the other hand, the daughters of Jerusalem are mocking Shulamite—"What is your beloved more than another beloved?"— as they make fun of her and blame her for making such ado about him. You see, the worldly heart sees nothing excellent or special in the Lord Jesus. They see nothing important about His person, His position, His doctrine, or His blessing.

Jesus said to the Laodicean church, the lukewarm church of the last days, "Behold, I stand at the door and knock. If anyone hears My voice and opens the door, I will come in to him and dine with him, and he with Me" (Rev. 3:20). Christ is on the outside. If He were on the inside, our comfort zone would be invaded, and our convenience would be challenged to commitment. In the last days, intimacy with Christ is replaced with cultural and political correctness. Blending in with the world = lukewarm. Be sure you are not asleep.

12

Boom! This is My Man

Song of Songs 5:10–16

SOLOMON AND SHULAMITE ARE in the midst of marital adjustment. Solomon knocks on the door, she won't let him in, she gets up to open the door, he is gone, so she looks for him and seeks help from the daughters of Jerusalem. In response, the daughters ask, "What is so great about your husband? Why should we be concerned? Why should we help you find him?" Shulamite answers their sarcastic questions and points out in detail why Solomon is so special to her—no one can compare to her lover, and no man completes her soul like this man.

Verse 10

This verse speaks of Solomon's royalty. He is distinguished among ten thousand.

In the following verses, Shulamite begins to describe specific features of Solomon.

Verse 11

Solomon's head is like gold that is both precious and fine. The Hebrew word means "fine gold guarded as a jewel, a gold that is pure and free from all inferior metals."

From his neck upwards, his hair is like rolling hill country. It forms waves in lines as hill upon hill. The color is in strong contrast to his skin because his hair is very black.

Verse 12

"His eyes are like doves by the rivers of water, washed with milk"— In other words, his pupils are swimming in the clear whites of his eyes.

Verse 13

She describes his cheeks as a flower bed planted with sweet scented flowers and says precious liquid myrrh drips from his lips.

Verse 14

His hands and nails are tanned and strong, very distinct. His body is like a work of art to her, made of ivory with sapphires placed in it.

Verse 15

His entire aspect is as majestic as the Lebanon towering over Galilee and precious like the choice cedars.

Verse 16

Shulamite says that his speech radiates only sweet utterances. No stature of an emperor could warrant higher acclaim. Her final words signify that she has fully answered in minute detail and grand hyperbole the teasing question of her friends. No wonder she risked her reputation to seek him! No wonder she subpoenaed her friends to inform him of her passion. No wonder she is pledged to him for life.

She concludes her description to the doubting daughters of Jerusalem by saying, "This, ladies, this one is my lover . . . this is my friend!" or in other words, "Boom! This is my man, ladies. Who do you have?"

More Than Sex

Their relationship was deeper than sexual attraction. There was companionship and comradeship. They were friends who enjoyed each other's fellowship deeply.

Some years ago, a pastor was driving through a particularly beautiful part of Tennessee with an English evangelist. Suddenly this evangelist, overcome by the glorious beauty of the scenery, burst out in a loud voice and with an expressive gesture of his hands said, "Well done, Lord!" Such emotion stirs the soul of Shulamite at the thought of her beloved.

She was cut off from him and wanted to renew the closeness she once experienced.

SOLOMON AND CHRIST

Verse 10

"White and ruddy"—"White" speaks of purity and holiness; "ruddy" is a symbol of health.

With regards to Christ, this speaks of purity and passion held in perfect balance in His life. He attracted men, won the adoration of women, and drew little children to Himself. All sin, all suggestiveness, all temptation simply withered and died in His presence.

"White" also points to Christ's divine glory. In Him we may behold the beauty of the Lord. His love to us renders Him lovely. He is "white" in the spotlessness of His life.

"Ruddy" reminds us of the bloody suffering He went through at His death. And it also reminds us of His assuming the nature of man—Adam means "red earth."

He has a loveliness that is found in no one else for He is "chief among ten thousand." In the Apostle John's vision of Christ, we see the throne of God, high and lifted up, with God Himself seated there, surrounded by the full circle rainbow of emerald and ringed by heaven's admiring throng. We see into the spotlight of glory, purer than the crystal stream that flows from the throne of God. He is the Lion of the tribe of Judah, the root of David, the Lamb of Calvary. As He takes the scroll, the title deed of the planet Earth, from Him who sits upon the throne, the heavenly hosts burst into song. There are ten thousand times ten thousand and Jesus is the Chief of them all.

Verse 11—Head

"Gold" symbolizes sovereignty. Christ has sovereign dominion over all. He is sovereign over His Church and all its members. Our Lord put aside the splendor that was His before the worlds began when He entered into human life as a man among men.

He was born of royal stock, of David's line; even though outwardly seeming to be but a Galilean peasant, raised as a laboring man to work at a carpenter's bench, royal dignity clung to Him as a kingly robe. The demons acknowledged it. Peter saw it—"Thou are the Christ! The Son of the living God." Thou art the Lord's anointed. The hosts of heaven acknowledge it.

"Locks are wavy, and black as a raven" speaks of strength, and it denotes that he is ever young and there is in him nothing that waxes old. He is the same yesterday, today, and forever.

The secret of Samson's great strength lay in his Nazarite hair. Samson, shorn of his locks, was as weak as a kitten. Samson with that hair tumbling down to his shoulders could tear a lion in two. Samson, in the power of his strength, could pick up the gates of Gaza and carry them off to the hills outside of town. So it was with our Lord—He was strong, so very strong. Men could nail Him to a tree, but that was only because He allowed it. They could lock Him in a tomb and put Caesar's seal upon it, but when the prophesied three days and three nights were over, He arose, heaved the gates of hell upon His massive shoulders, and burst forth from the domain of death in mighty triumph.

Verse 12—Eyes

"His eyes" are gentle and kind. Those eyes who gazed out over nothingness before the worlds began; those eyes who saw the universe throw its web of stars and galaxies into place; those eyes who beheld the first glimpse of light and the first mountain and valley; those eyes who saw life explode upon the earth; and those eyes who saw the first man and first woman.

This is the one who created it all, who cast the stars into place and gave them each names; He is the one who breathed life into that human clay and man became a living soul.

The eyes of Christ read the soul of Judas and saw the blood money in his purse, hidden away beneath the folds of his robe, and knew of the wretched traitor's eternal doom. Those eyes looked upon Peter, the eyes that filled Peter with agony of soul, filled with bitter remorse, went out to his own Gethsemane in utter anguish. Those same eyes that glowed with fellowship on the resurrection day, now gaze upon us from glory and see us wherever we are; He looks upon us—the joy of His heart.

These are the same eyes which will gaze into ours when we see Him face to face—"Open our eyes, Lord; we want to see Jesus."

Verse 13—Tongue

No one ever spoke like Jesus. His words "are sweet to the taste . . . like honeycomb." Jeremiah said that His words were found and he ate them . . . and they were sweet to the taste.

Verse 14—Hands

Great men had their hands adorned with gold rings set with precious stones, but in Shulamite's eyes, Solomon's hands themselves were as gold rings.

Think of the hands of Jesus, the hands He placed on the heads of little children, the hands that touched the casket of the widow's son so that the dead man leaped to life, and the hands He placed so warmly upon the leper.

O how we need a touch today from the Master. O Lord, touch us today. Anoint us today with the touch of Your hand. One day all will see the precious pierced hands of our Savior and Lord.

His body reminds us of the incarnation of Christ—God becoming man. His body which He kept in subjection to His Father's will even unto death.

Verse 15—Legs

"His legs are pillars of marble" reminds us of His stability and steadfastness.

On the cross, Jesus carried the weight of the sin of the whole world. "For He made Him who knew no sin to be sin for us" (2 Cor. 5:21). He stood firm against the unrighteousness and the temptation of Satan himself.

Even on the cross the soldiers dare not break His legs.

Verses 15b–16

To those who believe He is precious, and He is altogether lovely. O to behold His face, to look into His eyes.

"I am my beloved and my beloved is mine . . . Let him kiss me with the kisses of his mouth." Shulamite says, "Daughters of Jerusalem, 'this is my beloved, and this is my friend.'"

PRACTICAL APPLICATION

Let's learn from Shulamite's experience. She rejected her beloved's desire to have close fellowship and intimacy. She realized her mistake, and she begins the process to recover her failed relationship. She turns for help from the daughters of Jerusalem and asks them to help her find her beloved. She says that if you find Him, tell him my heart is yearning for him; tell him I repent of my indifference, of my cold-heartedness and my unconcern, and I want him above everything else.

Christian, is this the cry of your heart? "Oh, that I knew where I might find him!" (Job 23:3)

Tell the Lord "I am lovesick; my whole being is yearning after You; I want to be restored to You, to the sweetness of communion."

When the daughters of Jerusalem finally understand why Solomon meant so much to Shulamite, they respond by saying, "Where has he gone? How is it that you have let him slip out of your sight if he is so much to you?" (paraphrase of Song of Songs 6:1).

13

No Ordinary Man
Song of Songs 6:1–9

ONCE AGAIN, SHULAMITE FINDS herself searching throughout the city to find her beloved Solomon. She is remorseful that she rejected and turned away her beloved, her friend.

In the previous chapter, she asked the daughters of Jerusalem for help in finding the one who has her heart, and they sarcastically asked her what was so impressive about her beloved and why they should bother looking for him. Shulamite then described the beauty, wonder, majesty, and awe of her beloved. Shulamite's description of Solomon aroused their interest, and they are now eager to help her in her search for him.

Indeed, Solomon is no ordinary husband. He is no ordinary man. He is no ordinary lover. They now see why he is so special to her above all others.

Verse 1

The daughters of Jerusalem ask, "Where has he gone? How is it that you have let him slip out of your sight if he means so much to you?"

Verses 2–3

"My beloved has gone to his garden" means that Solomon has suddenly reappeared as Shulamite speaks, for the garden is Shulamite herself (4:12–15; 5:1). They are reunited, and verse 3 declares that they belong to each other.

In verses 4–10, Solomon praises his wife and shows his unconditional acceptance of Shulamite despite any marital challenges, adjustments, or problems.

Verse 4

Solomon begins in verse 4 to compare Shulamite with two of the most beautiful places in Israel. Tirzah was a beautiful oasis, later to become the first capital of the Northern Kingdom (1 Kings 14:17; 15:21, 33; 16:8, 23), and Jerusalem was the City of God.

Shulamite's beauty is as awesome as an army about to enter into battle, fully confident of victory. Solomon is totally vanquished by her beauty and loveliness.

Verse 5a

He cries out against the overcoming nature of her look. The word *overcome* means "overwhelmed." The idea means to press overpoweringly against one, to infuse terror. Such are the effects of Shulamite's beauty on her husband.

Verses 5b–7

Solomon repeats these words to her despite their misunderstanding the other night. These are the same words he spoke to her on their wedding night. Solomon still treats her the same because showing his love for her is not based on her performance. He loves her now as much as he loved her on their wedding night. To him, she is still as beautiful as a bride, and his love is still unchanged.

Verses 8–9

Solomon compares Shulamite to the other women in the palace. In Solomon's eyes, his precious wife has more to offer than all the women of the kingdom.

Shulamite towered over all the so-called glamour girls of their day. Solomon preferred her. He chose her. He loved her. He would give all he had for her. He loved her . . . and her alone.

APPLICATION FOR THE CHRISTIAN

Verse 1

The daughters of Jerusalem asked a very proper question. Once they understood how precious the beloved was, they were perplexed how Shulamite could so easily let him slip through her fingers.

Often times when the world understands how precious Christ is, they look at the complacent Christian, the cultural Christian, the convenient Christian, the lukewarm Christian, the one who is straddling the fence with one foot in the world of compromise and the other trying to be religiously Christian. And they ask, "If Christ is so precious to you, if He means so much to you, why is it that you so easily allow fellowship to be broken? Why do you so readily permit other things to come in and hinder communion with Christ? Why have you been silent about Him? Please tell us more so we may find him too."

As we present Christ to the world, they will ask how they can find our Shepherd, our Beloved for themselves. We are reminded of the very first question in the New Testament—The wise men from the east came into Jerusalem asking, "Where is He that is born King of the Jews?"

Our witness and testimony cause others to ask us to tell them how to find our Beloved.

Verses 2–3

Solomon simply appears, and there is a declaration of mutual commitment. This reminds us that Jesus will never leave us nor forsake us, even when we think He is gone, He is really there. For He Himself has said, "I will never leave you nor forsake you" (Heb. 13:5).

Paul said it this way—"For I am persuaded that neither death nor life, nor angels nor principalities nor powers, nor things present nor things to come, nor height nor depth, nor any other created thing, shall be able to separate us from the love of God which is in Christ Jesus our Lord" (Rom. 8:38–39).

It doesn't matter what you are facing today, or what you are feeling today, or what you are fearing today, Jesus is there with you. And like He said to the stormy waters of the Galilee, He will say to the storms of your life, "Peace be still." Jesus is there in the rocky boat with you. If it seems so long and the waves are seemingly getting higher and higher and you think you are about to drown, remember He is there, and He will not forsake you.

Verses 4–9

Solomon repeats the words spoken on their wedding night and assures Shulamite of his love, that he loves her now as much as he loved her on the wedding night. To him, she is still as beautiful as a bride, his love is still unchanged, and she is not treated as being on a performance basis.

This reminds us that there is nothing that we can do to cause Christ to love us more than He already does. He loves us beyond measure. He loved us first, therefore we love Him (1 John 4:19).

Like the prodigal's father who lovingly and patiently waited for his wayward son to return, so it is with our Lord who lovingly waits for us to come home and have sweet fellowship once again.

You can be busy like Martha trying to please the Lord by her busy work, desiring the Lord to notice her. Or you can be like Mary who chose the better part and sat at the Master's feet. O yes there is a time to work, and there is a time to sit at His feet. But remember,

He loves you unconditionally, no matter what the circumstances may be.

If you are wayward, just as a loving father will patiently discipline his son, so it is with our heavenly father. But you are still his child.

It is better to have communion with Him than to break fellowship.

He loves you even if you misunderstand, like Shulamite who misunderstood, yet Solomon loved her unconditionally.

"I am my beloved's, and my beloved is mine" (6:3); I am Christ's, and Christ is mine. Nothing can separate us from His love.

Christ chose you. He prefers you. He loves you. He would give all that He has for you; in fact, He did give all that He had (Eph. 1:3–7).

14

Homesick

Song of Songs 6:10–13

IN THIS REFLECTION, SHULAMITE goes down to the royal walnut gardens to reflect on the beauty and vegetation now beginning to blossom.

Verse 10

As she returns to the palace, she runs into the daughters of Jerusalem who ask her this question. Shulamite appears as the morning sunrise that breaks through the darkness of the night sky. She is beautiful like the silvery white moon, pure as the warm sun. The idea is that everything emphasizes the freshness of the woman.

Shulamite responds . . .

Verses 11–12

On this spring morning, she had gone down to look at what reminded her of her home. We must remember that this farm girl was quickly elevated from a country peasant girl to being the wife of the King of Israel.

We derive from these verses that she had not fully accultur-
ated to the city life—to the royal life of the palace. So, she goes to
this place that reminds her of her home. We understand this more
fully as we look at verse 13.

Verse 13

For the first time in the Song, Shulamite is addressed by name. The
name *Shulamite* is not really her name, but it points to her place
of origin.

Shulamite is from the town of Shunem, known later as
Shulem (the "l" and "n" sounds often interchanged in Hebrew and
Semitic languages). Today, this town is called Sulam.

Background of Shunem:

1. Shunem was a town of the tribe of Issachar (Josh. 19:17, 18).

2. Located at the foot of the Hill of Moreh, also known as the
   Little Hermon.

3. Shunem was noted for its beautiful woman (Abishag,
   1 Kings 1:3–4).

4. Elisha's hostess lived there (the Shulamite woman, 2 Kings
   4:8–11).

Thus, Shulamite was from Shunem or Shulem and was a
member of the tribe of Issachar. Her home was in Galilee. Her
name gives us the location of her origin and provides the feminine
of the name "Solomon."

The imaginary daughters of Jerusalem are desirous to look
upon her (Song of Songs 6:13), which means to gaze or delight, to
feast one's eyes upon her. In response, Shulamite asks them why.
"What would you see in the Shulamite—as it was, the dance of the
two camps?"

The word *return* can simply mean "turn or leap", having the
idea of whirling.

The "two camps" refers to a double camp or a divided line-up of dancers, musicians, and other participants that would sing or chant.

Shulamite is very humble and still fails to fully comprehend her own beauty and the effect it has on others, especially on her husband.

Remember now that the daughters of Jerusalem are imaginary. What really is taking place here is that Solomon is asking Shulamite to dance for him. This is a graceful and intimate dance he is requesting of her and in Chapter Seven he describes what he sees. Shulamite and Solomon, after their misunderstanding, are once again in sweet reunion and harmony as husband and wife.

FOR THE CHRISTIAN

This section reminds us of at least three important points.

1. Shulamite represents the Church, the bride of Christ. Therefore, her presence in the walnut garden, reflecting and yearning for her home, is a picture of the Christian's desire for heaven.

   You see, she was homesick. The palace and all the worldly pleasures, temptations, trials, and expectations were not really hers. She was not comfortable with all the worldly pomp and clamor. So, Shulamite is thinking about her home—yearning to be with her family, her church family, her home, namely heaven.

   Does your heart yearn for heaven? The Scriptures teach that believers are "strangers and pilgrims on the earth;" that we are "sojourners and pilgrims" (Heb. 11:13; 1 Peter 2:11). A Christian is not very comfortable here in this world; His heart will yearn to be with God's people and to ponder the splendor, glory, and majesty of heaven and heaven's Christ. Believers think about the glories and excitements associated with heaven.

2. Verse 13 reminds us that as the daughters of Jerusalem (actually, it is Solomon) desired to look upon Shulamite as she gracefully dances, one day God will put us on display before the whole universe and all of creation to behold our beauty (Eph. 2:7).

   The bride of Christ will be for the demonstration of God's grace throughout all the ages. All of the created universe is going to see us. None of us is worthy to be there, but we are going to be there because we are in Christ. It is because He loved us and gave Himself for us. We will be there for His glory and for our good. Can you think of anything better than that?

3. Shulamite's self-deprecation of "what would you see" reminds me of Isaiah who beheld the glory of the Lord in the temple and stated, "Woe is me, for I am undone! Because I am a man of unclean lips" (Isa. 6:5).

   And Peter, after seeing the miracle of the catching of fish and recognizing the holiness of Christ, fell down at the Lord's knees and said, "Depart from me, for I am a sinful man, O Lord" (Luke 5:8). And Paul who stated, "O wretched man that I am! Who will deliver me from this body of death? I thank God—it is through Jesus Christ our Lord!" (Rom. 7:24–25). And John the Apostle on the Isle of Patmos, who turning around and seeing the majesty of the Lord, fell to his face as a dead man.

   We don't deserve God's grace. We don't deserve God's love. We don't deserve His mercy. We don't deserve a home in heaven. However, we read, "There is therefore now no condemnation to those who are in Christ Jesus" (Rom. 8:1).

There is nothing in us that is beautiful or holy or just, but God sees us as beautiful and will show us off before the whole universe one day. God loved us first, therefore we love Him. And like Shulamite, we are amazed that our Beloved thinks we are lovely.

FOR MARRIED COUPLES

You are not perfect, and your spouse is not perfect. You have faults, and your spouse has faults. You try to strengthen any weak area in your life, but you must understand, that on this side of heaven, for all your effort—no matter how sincere—neither you nor your spouse will reach perfection.

Some things cannot be changed. So, where does this leave us?

1. Choose to accept your spouse the way he or she is.

2. Choose to accept your spouse the way he or she is: even knowing all their faults, imperfections, and weaknesses.

3. Choose not to dwell upon those weaknesses.

4. Choose instead to dwell upon, enjoy, and even celebrate the strengths, positive qualities, and beauties of your spouse.

5. Choose not to irritate or become aggravated every time some fault or weakness comes to the surface.

6. Choose to give that to the Lord.

7. Choose that you will love your spouse the way he or she is and that you will not condemn him or her.

8. Choose not to become angry with him or her.

9. Choose to decline trying to take out the speck in the eye of your spouse until the beam in your own eye has been removed (Luke 6:41–42).

Realize you are imperfect, and your spouse is imperfect. Give your spouse the joy of knowing that you accept them unconditionally.

15

Dancing
Song of Songs 7:1–13

Verses 1–13

THE DANCING HAS BEGUN. The daughters of Jerusalem had urged Shulamite to dance in 6:13. Remember now, that because the daughters of Jerusalem are imaginary, it was really Solomon asking her to dance.

So now she is dancing before Solomon alone. As Shulamite dances before him, Solomon begins to detail the beauties of his wife. Every detail suggests motion of the beautiful curves and contours of her form.

Verses 1–4

Her royal bearing is so apparent to Solomon he calls her "O prince's daughter." He compares her with the beauty of nature, spices, fine jewels, fruit, wine, and ivory.

Verse 5

She is majestic, and her hair appears as a red-purple color. Solomon is totally captivated by her and sees himself as a prisoner in the tresses of her hair.

Verse 8

Following this graceful and intimate dance of Shulamite before her husband, romantic intimacy begins, and in verse 8 Solomon is viewed as climbing the palm tree as he and Shulamite embrace.

The idea is that of securing the possession and the enjoyment of what the dance had promised.

Verse 9

In verse 9, Shulamite seemingly interrupts Solomon in midsentence and blends her sense of yearning with his. She calls Solomon by her pet name for him—"my beloved."

"The wine goes down smoothly" implies that, like good wine that has been sipped throughout an evening, the pleasing satisfaction of love still hovers long after they have gone to sleep. Shulamite seems to say it is time for sustained solitude and unhurried love.

She declares herself to belong to Solomon alone, just as Solomon's desire is only for her. Her devoted heart and impassioned instincts for Solomon will kindle his memory and stretch his imagination.

REGARDING THE CHURCH

This chapter reminds me of the beauty and glory of the Church.

Verse 1

Sandals

Shulamite wore sandals.

Think of the first thing the father put on the prodigal when he returned from his wandering ways. The prodigal was brought into the house, his feet shod as proof of acceptance and his right to draw near.

When Moses stood before God at the burning bush, God told him to take off his shoes for he was standing on Holy Ground. Moses was to keep his distance and not be so familiar or not take lightly that he was in the presence of God.

This reminds us of the Church, her standing and steps, when she makes contact with the world. Whenever and wherever we make contact with this present evil world, our feet should be "shod . . . with the preparation of the gospel of peace" (Eph. 6:15). The Scriptures also state, "How beautiful are the feet of those who preach the gospel of peace, who bring glad tidings of good things!" (Rom. 10:15).

Solomon mentions Shulamite's thighs. In Scripture, the thigh is associated with strength. When Jacob wrestled with the angel, he was able to maintain his own with the carnal, natural strength that was his until the mighty Wrestler reached out and touched Jacob's thigh. In that moment, Jacob's thigh was put out of joint, and he could not fight. He was a broken man. The only thing he could do was cling to this one who came from heaven. Only after all his natural strength was gone could he enter into spiritual power to walk henceforth with God.

Solomon's reference to Shulamite's thigh also reminds us that, when Christ comes back to reign, He will have His sword girded on His thigh—the symbol of power and strength. So, Solomon thus describes her with beauty and strength.

Verse 2

Navel

The "navel" reminds us of independent life. Once we were mysteriously wrapped in another's life and in due time, in due season, we were brought to birth and given an independent life of our own. Our navel remains as a reminder of that previous life mystery, just as the Church was a hidden mystery in the Old Testament and not revealed until the proper time, in due time, in due season, on the day of Pentecost.

There were many types, symbols, shadows, and indications of the Church in the womb of the Old Testament. Think of the stories of Joseph, Isaac, Rebekah, Ruth, Boaz, the Tabernacle, and the Psalms and Prophets, but yet the Church was hidden and not revealed until New Testament times. Solomon knew nothing about the Church, but the Holy Spirit did.

The "blended beverage" reminds us of new wine, a symbol of the Church. Jesus said that no man would put new wine into old wineskins lest they would burst (Matt. 9:17). Therefore, when the day of Pentecost was fully come, a new vessel was prepared to receive the new wine of the Spirit of God, and the Church was birthed.

"Your waist is a heap of wheat"—Wheat is also a symbol of the Church (Matt. 13:24–43).

Verse 4

Solomon said, "Your eyes like the pools in Heshbon by the gate of Bath Rabbim." Solomon saw something desirable.

Heshbon was originally a Moabite town, conquered by Moses and converted into a Levitical city. Levitical cities were scattered throughout the promised land for the tribe of Levi, which had been consecrated to serve God. The Levites were to act as a sanctifying influence on the Hebrew people.

Heshbon itself was about twenty miles east of the Jordan River, not far from where the river flows into the Dead Sea. The Dead Sea region is a barren wilderness. However, Heshbon was situated at the site of an excellent spring making it particularly desirable. A couple of pools stood at the gate of this city. It was a most beautiful sight.

You see, the Church is to be in the world—an oasis in the desert, a life-giving pool of delight and refreshment in a barren wilderness. The Church is to be something more desirable, a Levitical city, a haven of rest, a place of refreshment, a place where God is found in a hostile world.

May we as the Church "humble [ourselves], . . . seek [God's] face, and turn from [our] wicked ways, then [God] will hear from heaven, and will forgive [our] sin and heal [our] land" (2 Chron. 7:14).

Verses 8–13

For Married Couples

When reading this chapter, we are brought to an obvious understanding. Think about these phrases:

- *I will take hold of its branches*
- *I am my beloveds' and his desire is toward me*
- *Come, my beloved*
- *Let us go forth*
- *Let us lodge in the villages*
- *Let us get up early*
- *Let us see*
- *I will give you my love*
- *At our gates are pleasant fruits*
- *I have laid up for you, my beloved*

It doesn't take a rocket scientist to understand the exclusivity of their love for each other. Another word for "exclusivity" would be loyalty.

Loyalty

I am a loyalist. I am very loyal to my friends, I believe that my word is my bond, and a handshake is as complete as a contract. And I trust my friends to reciprocate loyalty.

To experience betrayal is a devastating thing to a loyalist. Christ experienced betrayal; and probably you have too at one time or another if you have lived long enough.

What we see here in Chapter Seven is an emphasis on loyalty. The full appreciation of and understanding of the unity of marriage is foundational to the practice of loyalty. A verbal attack on your spouse is a verbal attack on you. The same is true for a physical attack or a failure to nurture or a failure to please.

The positive corollary is that a choice to keep your mouth shut when tempted to say something against your spouse is a protection of yourself and therefore a benefit to you. The deliberate pleasuring, benefiting, and delighting of your spouse will benefit you. The both of you are one; therefore, you are, if you will, a joint being. What hurts your spouse hurts you, what benefits your spouse benefits you, and what pleases your spouse pleases you.

Those reasons alone provide a logical and practical basis for loyalty. Add to those realities the choice to love your spouse and the choice to obey the Lord with respect to God's commands for speech, behavior, attitude, roles, and responsibilities in marriage and you have an irrefutable case for absolute loyalty. Loyalty is a major component in a very successful, healthy, happy marriage.

Areas of loyalty that should be evident between husband and wife:

1. Loyalty regarding physical/sexual fidelity to your spouse.

    It is obvious according to Scripture that we are not to commit adultery (Ex. 20:14; Matt. 15:19; Rom. 7:2–3, et al).

It would be wise not to even touch someone in a way that would cause a person to stumble or dwell upon any portion of your body or to misunderstand your intention.

Spend quality time in the Word of God and in prayer to acknowledge afresh your utter dependence upon the Lord to walk righteously.

Remember Jesus said that apart from Him we can do nothing (John 15:5).

2. Loyalty regarding romantic affection solely for your spouse.

Do not withhold your affections from your spouse, and, by all means, make the choice that you will not for one second direct any amorous feelings, thoughts, or affections toward anyone besides your spouse (2 Cor. 10:5).

Just as we create "to-do" lists for good organization and to prioritize our day, we must affirmatively pray for, plan for, and prioritize things pertaining to the family. That "to-do" list should include how you can give your unrestricted affection to your spouse today. You should start doing this right now.

3. Loyalty regarding emotional dependence only upon your spouse.

The strongest marriages are those wherein each spouse recognizes that he or she needs the other. It is not a sign of weakness that you need your spouse. Indeed, recognizing your personal need for your spouse makes your marriage stronger.

An act of disloyalty would be allowing the development of an emotional dependence upon anyone besides your spouse. Do not allow some type of emotional dependence upon someone of the opposite gender to develop.

The safest practice is to not be alone with a person of the opposite sex.

4. Loyalty regarding keeping your confidences and private matters absolutely confidential and private.

You have violated the trust of your spouse and you have become disloyal if you reveal private matters with a third party. Countless private, secret, and confidential matters have been disclosed to someone other than a spouse in the name of sharing a "prayer request." Be careful not to do that.

Laws and rules of ethical conduct require confidentiality between certain types of persons, e.g. attorney-client, pastor-church member, etc. Serious consequences follow if that confidentiality is breached, and the damage is quite severe. The marriage relationship is far more important and deserves that type of confidentiality. Guard those confidences, secrets, and private matters with your life. It is that important. Do not rationalize an exception to such loyalty to your spouse.

5. Loyalty regarding immediately defending the person, character, and honor of your spouse and refusing to put down or demean your spouse.

    When anyone challenges the person, character, honor, intelligence, or motives of your spouse, you must immediately defend your spouse in order to be truly loyal to your spouse. When anyone ridicules, jests, or makes your spouse the object of a joke, immediately and without hesitation defend them.

    We reap sweet dividends when we have an open relationship with our spouse in complete and uncompromising commitment, defending one another no matter what.

6. Loyalty regarding being always united with your spouse in all communications with your children and in disciplining your children.

    Agree together to the rules and consequences of actions and discipline formulas regarding your children. Never disagree in front of the children. Discuss disagreements privately. Never have a child play one parent against the other. List the rules on the refrigerator. Discuss them with your children so they fully understand what the boundaries are. Discuss parenting together with your spouse.

7. Loyalty regarding keeping your spouse, rather than anyone else, as your confidante.

By putting your heads together, you combine your strengths. No person is without blind spots. Because spouses know each other and have an intimate relationship and communications, they are in the ideal position to be the confidante of the other. (Solomon also instructs us concerning the value of obtaining counsel from wise people—Prov. 11:14; 12:15; 15:22; 19:20; 20:18; 27:9.)

8. Loyalty regarding assisting, encouraging, and promoting your spouse to reach his or her full potential.

You are a team. Cheer each other on to your full potential. When you do, you win.

16

As Strong as Death

Song of Songs 8:1–7

Because of Shulamite's longing for home, she asks Solomon to come with her to visit her home for two purposes:

1. To renew the love covenant in the very place where their courtship began; and

2. To have a romantic rendezvous there which they could not have had before since they were obviously unmarried when they were courting.

In Song of Songs 7:11, she makes her request to visit home. She said the vineyards have budded, the grape blossoms are open, the pomegranates are in bloom, and the mandrakes give off a fragrance. Shulamite is saying, "Honey, spring is in the air, and love is calling us home to the place where we began. Let's go to the Galilee." And so they traveled north from Jerusalem.

Verse 1

In the ancient Middle East, public displays of affection were frowned on except in the case of certain family members. Thus, Shulamite wished that her husband were like a brother to her so that it would be acceptable to display her affection for him at any time.

Verse 2

Here we find that Shulamite plays different roles in the marriage.

She playfully assumes the role of an older sister—"I would lead you and bring you." The idea is of a superior leading an inferior, like in an older sister role. She even playfully assumes the role of a mother since the lady of the house would give special wine to the guests.

The Song also portrays the lovers as friends (5:1, 16). Solomon and Shulamite had a multifaceted relationship. They were lovers, friends, and at times like a brother and sister.

Verses 3–4

In verse 3 we find as his wife she desired his caresses, and in verse 4 once again, Shulamite gives the warning to refrain from romantic and intimate feelings and situations until you are married.

Feelings like hers are not to be toyed with, so great their explosive power, so painful their consequences if the marriage covenant is not their context. Abstinence is always in vogue until marriage.

Verse 5

Here we have a final picture presented of the couple.

The wilderness or desert have two symbolic meanings in the Old Testament.

1. The wilderness wanderings of Israel for forty years
   The idea is that the couple had overcome the various trials that threatened their relationship:
   a. Insecurity of Shulamite (1:5, 6).
   b. The foxes in their marriage (2:15).
   c. Indifference (5:2–7).

2. God's curse (Jer. 22:6; Joel 2:3)

The fact that the couple is coming up from the wilderness implies they had overcome the curse of disunity, disharmony, and dysfunction.

It also means that they probably traveled by way of the Jericho Road, through the Jordan Valley, passing through Bet Shean Pass to Shunem. This was the very same route Shulamite took when she went to Jerusalem in the wedding procession.

They finally arrive in familiar territory; they come to the apple tree where she first won his love. This tree witnessed her birth and the beginning of their love together. The apple tree was also sometimes used as a symbol of love and romance in the ancient world.

Notice she says, "I awakened you under the apple tree." It is debated whether either Solomon, Shulamite, or even a so-called relative spoke these words. Nevertheless, this is a metaphor for new life or rather a new way of perceiving life, which their love has brought to them. Much as he or she was the product of the parents' love and was brought into the world by physical birth, they had now received a second birth or awakening through the love they had given each other.

One purpose for this trip was to renew the love covenant, and that is done as Shulamite speaks in verses 6 and 7.

Verses 6–7

"Set me as a seal upon your heart and arm." A "seal" indicates ownership. She wants to be Solomon's most prized and precious possession. He should possess her in such a way so as to never separate himself from her. She asked to be her lover's most valued possession, a possession that would influence two areas:

1. His thoughts ("upon your heart")

2. His actions ("upon your arm")

The rest of verse 6 and including verse 7 sums up the nature and power of the love depicted in the Song.

"Love is as strong as death." Love is as universal and irresistible as death. Death is seen here as being powerful and nothing can withstand it (Jer. 9:21). Against death nothing can hold its ground or escape. All must eventually yield to it.

The type of love Shulamite describes is as powerful as death, for it too can seize men with irresistible force. The idea is that whomever death attacks must die, and whomever love attacks must love. As death kills in relationship to everything living, even so love kills in relationship to everything else that is not the object of one's love. In other words, love is very exclusive—there is only room for one love.

"Jealousy as cruel as the grave" means just as the grave takes full possession of the dead (Ps. 49:13–15), so does jealousy burn against everyone who will try to violate the right of ownership.

"Its flames are flames of fire, a most vehement flame." Those flames will keep burning under any circumstances that threaten love. "A most vehement flame" is a superlative expression, as strong as anything Hebrew can kindle, to show the brilliance and tenacity of love. It means the flame of Yah, that is, of Yahweh. This kind of love, the record states, is the very flame of Jehovah. In Hebrew this is the flame of the most vehement kind, a flame of bright shining and fiery flashes.

Love of the right kind is not a flame kindled by man, but by God. This is the only place in the book where God is mentioned. He is the source of this love, and before Him the love covenant is renewed.

Verse 7

This verse tells us that nothing can quench this kind of love. There isn't enough money in the world to buy such love. This is a special kind of love; a love that the world cannot produce. Any attempt to buy love depersonalizes it.

"If love is priceless, how then can it be obtained?" The answer is that it must be given. And ultimately love is a gift from God.

The rest of the chapter explains how this couple received the priceless gift of love.

FOR THE CHRISTIAN

Because of strict social conventions, oftentimes a bride and bridegroom were kept apart. It would have been highly improper for Shulamite, under the rigid code of the day, to have expressed her love for Solomon in public and in an open way. However, it would not have been improper to embrace her brother. This is why she says, "Oh, that you were like my brother." How often we wish the same thing regarding our Lord. We are living in a world where social customs can be strong.

In our culture, it is quite acceptable for a person to go to a football game and yell, shout, cheer, wave his arms, and throw his hat in the air. Yet, our culture states it is quite out of place to get excited about the Lord. The moment a person expresses any religious emotion he is called a fanatic, Jesus freak, or a nut. A few unconventional souls go ahead and shout anyway. I believe most Christians wished they had that kind of courage.

Verse 3

This is the pinnacle of love for Christ. Have you ever felt like Shulamite? Have there been times when your longing for the Lord has welled up in inexpressible longing and desire? Have you ever felt like stepping on every social restraint and shouting from the rooftop, "My Jesus, I love you!"?

Verse 5

This verse reminds us that, although we do not know when, one of these days, Christ will come from seemingly out of nowhere. He will leave the clouds and "descend from heaven with a shout, with the voice of the archangel, and with the trumpet of God. And the dead in Christ will rise first. Then we who are alive and remain shall be caught up" (1 Thess. 4:16–17).

"I awakened you under the apple tree." Remember, under the apple tree is where Shulamite and Solomon, her Shepherd-king, first kindled their love and apparently where Shulamite or Solomon was born. This is where they met.

This phrase is a reminder to us that it is good for us to remember the place where we first met our great Shepherd-king, when we were born into the family of God, when life began. Some remember the exact time, date, and events. There are some who cannot remember the exact moment of their new birth, but they remember their love for Christ began to grow and unfold.

Verses 6–7

"A seal upon your heart *(your thoughts)* . . . upon your arm *(your actions).*" In ancient times the seal was a symbol of ownership and was used to make contracts. Rings are used in the same way today regarding marriage. When a young couple falls in love and they plan a future together, he presents her with an engagement ring. She wears it as a token of their intention to marry, a sign that her affections are completely engaged. She has given her hand to her beloved and, upon that hand, she wears the seal, the signet, the symbol of love.

In the same way, the Lord Jesus told us of His great love for us, a love that passes knowledge, a love that is so amazing. He wants to protect and provide for us, to be near and dear to us. He wants us to be His, to share His home, to reign with Him. The evident token of His great, magnificent love, He has given us an engagement ring. Paul said, "having believed, you were sealed with the Holy Spirit of promise, who is the guarantee of our inheritance" (Eph. 1:13–14). The Holy Spirit is Christ's seal, Christ's signet, the symbol of His love. We are pledged now to watch, wait, and work for Him; our hand and heart are His.

"Love is as strong as death" reminds us of the strength of Christ's love for us when He died on the cross for our sins. In fact, death could not hold him, He rose, victoriously over sin, death, the grave, and the power of hell. He conquered it all. Because He conquered death, sin, the grave, and hell, we who believe will also be victorious over sin, death, the grave, and the horrors of hell. Love is jealous; its flames are of fire, as the flames of God.

We read in the Ten Commandments that God said, "I, the Lord your God, am a jealous God" (Exod. 20:5). Because He loves you, He is jealous for you.

A spouse who truly loves will not encourage unfaithfulness. If one encourages unfaithfulness, they truly do not love. God loves us so much He does not want to see us turning away from the enjoyment of His love and trying to find satisfaction in any lesser affection, which can only be for harm and eventual ruin.

The end of these things is death: "The wages of sin is death" (Rom. 6:23).

Paul said to the Corinthians: "For I am jealous for you with godly jealousy. For I have betrothed you to one husband, that I may present you as a chaste virgin to Christ. But I fear, lest somehow, as the serpent deceived Eve by his craftiness, so your minds may be corrupted from the simplicity that is in Christ" (2 Cor. 11:2–3).

Verse 7

This verse reminds us of Christ's never-ending love for His children. The Scripture is replete with statements about God's forever love for those who believe. You see, love is what it is all about!

Love drew our Beloved down from the skies, love took Him to Calvary, and down into the regions of death. His was love, invincible love, the love that many waters cannot quench, that the floods can never drown. Love wins out in the end.

After the rapture of the Church, Satan will attack and take control of the Earth until that day, a few years later, when Jesus, the King of Kings and Lord of Lords, will return victoriously descending upon the Mount of Olives, which is the very same place He ascended 2,000 years ago.

He will defeat the enemies of God and establish His kingdom on Earth. Love will triumph at last. The day will come and nothing can keep Christ from being victorious.

CONCLUSION

1. Couples can overcome difficulties by remembering their first love and first dreams and remembering the future is as bright as the promises of God.

2. Christians must remember that God's love is never-ending. His love is strong, jealous, and enduring.

3. Those who endure to the end will reap blessings beyond measure.

17

Romantic Encounter
Song of Songs 8:8–14

FINALLY, SHULAMITE ARRIVES HOME with Solomon, and in verse 8 she is having a conversation with her brothers concerning her little sister.

Verse 8

We learn that Shulamite has a younger sister. "She has no breasts" means that her sister is still very young and without sexual development; therefore, at this time, there is no concern.

However, "what shall we do for our sister in the day when she is spoken for" refers to the day when suitors come courting her (1 Sam. 25:39).

Verse 9

The brothers respond to Shulamite's question. In the ancient Middle East, brothers often served as the nearest guardians and counselors of the sister in the area of marriage, even more so than the parents (Gen. 24:50–60; 34:1–17).

The brothers are saying that "if she proves to be a wall" or, in other words, inaccessible to seduction, she will be rewarded. The wall referred to here is one that stands firm and withstanding all immoral assaults. However, if she is a door, which although closed is built to be opened or accessible to seduction, then they will watch her in such a manner that no seducers will be able to approach her and thus protect her from promiscuity.

Verse 10

This conversation reminds Shulamite that she was pure when she entered into marriage with Solomon. The only difference was that Shulamite was fully developed and ready for love—but only with her husband. Shulamite kept her virginity and purity and was able to enter into a marriage covenant of peace with Solomon. So, Shulamite boasts with joy and pride that she passed the test. She came to the betrothal fully mature of form and figure, ripe and ready for marriage.

Notice the signs of maturation as God expresses His love for Jerusalem as found in Ezekiel 16:7–8. God looked upon Jerusalem with love and compassion.

"Then I became in his eyes as one who found peace." His eyes must refer to her husband; perhaps she nods or points to him as she speaks these words.

The "peace" that she "found" seems to follow through on the fortress imagery of "wall" and "towers." It speaks of complete security and total well-being, which she has discovered and carried with her to the marriage.

The Hebrew *Shalom* is a wordplay on Shulamite, Jerusalem, and Solomon. All three have the same three consonants "sh", "l", and "m." To the relationship, she has brought beauty, purity, and strength like Jerusalem (6:4, 13; 8:11).

Verse 11

This verse implies that either Shulamite is asking Solomon to reward her brothers from his wealth for taking care of her when she was young or she is thanking them for their faithfulness.

In other words, Shulamite is taking care of her family from her newfound wealth since she married Solomon. Or this is a reference to the fact that the brothers may have worked for Solomon, thus explaining Shulamite working in the vineyard where Solomon and she first met.

Verse 12

Shulamite says to Solomon, "My own vineyard is before me." She is saying that only she could give herself to another. She uses her "own vineyard" to speak of her own person, which was hers to give, and she freely chose to give herself and all that she has to Solomon.

Verse 13

Shulamite's friends from her childhood are apparently in the house, having come to see her and to hear her singing. So, Solomon asks her to satisfy them and to sing. The intensity of their love for each other has not lessened; in fact it has intensified.

Verse 14

Shulamite begins her song as she leads Solomon outside leaving all the others behind in the house. They disappear into the flowered hills to practice outdoors that which they had come up north to do—to have a romantic encounter at the place where their love was kindled at the beginning. With this the Song of Solomon comes to an end.

The Song of Solomon is a beautiful picture of God's endorsement of physical love between husband and wife. Intense devotion and commitment to each other is emphasized. Taking delight in each other is a primary focus.

"For this reason a man will leave his father and mother, and will be joined to his wife. And they will become one flesh" (Gen. 2:24 (NLV)).

THE GREATEST LOVER

The Song of Songs shows us that the fulfillment of human sexuality is honorable in the context of marriage. Moral purity before marriage is praised. Premarital sex has no place in God's plans (2:7; 3:5). Faithfulness, before and after marriage, is expected and honored (6:3; 7:10; 8:12). Such faithfulness in marital love beautifully pictures God's love for and commitment to His people.

I find it interesting that Shulamite's zeal for her husband at the end again pushes her to take the initiative. The Song ends as it began with her arms stretched out to him in invitation.

Her bonded-ness to him reveals itself in her favorite name—"my Beloved" (1:13). She feels as close to him as can any kin to another. Her openness to him and her vulnerability to his passions becomes plain in the imagery of the gazelle and young stag (2:7, 8, 17). The strong eroticism of this language serves to ready both partners for their embrace. Her sense of the beauty of love's most intimate act is as alert as ever; she sees her body as more than flesh and bone—it's a veritable mountain range, alive with the fragrance of all the spices any palace could know (1:12–14; 4:13–14). The mutuality of their desire is clear; what she wants is what he wants (8:14; 4:6). They are both committed to the permanence of their love.

You see, the greatest lover of all knew the significance of this permanency: "Having loved His own who were in the world, He loved them to the end" (John 13:1). The couple in the Song would have admired that commitment.

Their love reminds us to look to our own love and, more importantly, to draw upon His.

What I also find interesting is that the story ends in a garden. Paradise has been regained. The Shepherd-king uses the word *dwell* literally meaning "to abide permanently." The idea is that never again will his bride be in danger from the world or any other enemy. She has come into his garden at last, there to remain in a paradise of bliss forever. He has no higher hope of happiness than to hear her voice. What can she say to him that he would want to hear? How about "Solomon, I love you, I love you, I love you"?

Our Shepherd, the Lord Jesus Christ, the uncreated eternal Son of the living God, He who has had the shining seraphim to be His servants, who fills all heaven with His praise, says to us, His bride, "let Me hear your voice. Let Me hear you sing, talk to Me, dwell with Me in paradise, and sing for Me." O how He longs to hear our voices even today. He loves to hear us raise our voice in songs of adoration and praise. He loves to hear our words of worship. But what can we say to the one who created all the stars, the planets, and the universe?

We have the Shepherd's last request: "Let me hear you sing," or, in other words, "Tell me you love me." Then Shulamite's final reply: "Make haste, my beloved, and be like a gazelle or a young stag on the mountains of spices."

She no longer talks about the mountains of separation (2:17)—those days are gone. She talks about the mountains of spices—or the scented slopes.

What would our Shepherd want us to say to Him that could exceed that? There is not a thing that could exceed that. "Make haste; Lord Jesus, come."

Come in all Your vigor and in the splendor of that boundless life of Yours.

Come! Leap over all obstacles! Let nothing ever come between us again.

The Song ends where the book of Revelation ends, where the Bible itself ends. "Make haste, my Beloved . . . Even so, come, Lord Jesus . . ."

CONCLUSION

1. Couples must develop a healthy and biblical attitude toward sexual union.

2. A biblical and healthy attitude will provide a good example for their children.

3. God's love is permanent and never fails.

4. Develop communication between each other.

5. Develop communication with God.

6. Study the Word and learn about God's love relationship with you.

7. Yearn for a personal, real, deep, and daily relationship with Christ.

18

Down Memory Lane

WE HAVE EMBRACED THE love story of Solomon and Shulamite. We followed them along the journey as they fell in love, meeting in the budding vineyards of northern Israel. And, with great interest, we peaked around the trees and shrubs observing them as they courted.

We rejoiced with them as we followed and participated in the wedding procession and observed the splendor and pomp of ceremony as soldiers and banners and shields glistened in the sunlight. The air was perfumed with myrrh and frankincense.

We beheld the mysterious, sensual, traveling bridal carriage that Solomon made out of purple, gold, and silver, with its interior paved with love.

We danced with them through the winding rolling hills and mountains and flowering valleys of the Galilee.

With our eyes wide open and full of wonder and excitement, we entered the marble walls, the golden outlines, and ivory accents of Solomon's palace in Jerusalem, the City of David, the City of God, Jerusalem, the Golden.

We walked discreetly and whispered in tones of ecstasy during their honeymoon. Sometime later, with great concern and a breaking heart, we witnessed their first misunderstanding.

And we traveled with Shulamite through the dark streets of the city as she put herself in danger, sacrificing her reputation and putting her life on the line. She was searching for her beloved Solomon and no one would help her. We wanted to help her. We understood why she was searching. Her friends finally understood, and no longer mocked Shulamite for what she was doing. They also began to search for her Shepherd-king, this One who was so amazing, this One so lovely, this One so majestic, this One who brings peace, joy, comfort, provision, and love.

We became so happy, so thrilled, so overwhelmed with joy as her beloved appeared seemingly out of nowhere and found her, embraced her, loved her, and cherished her, his chosen bride. No longer was Shulamite in danger. No longer will she be alone. No longer will she be in despair. No longer will she have a void in her life. No longer will her soul be empty. From now on, she will never again lock the door of her heart, keeping her beloved outside. Never again will she keep her beloved away from embracing her, loving her, caring for her, and protecting her. Never again will she turn Him away.

Then, we frolicked with them as they reunited and reconciled. We were there when they made up—when they forgave each other.

O, what a sweet reunion, like the prodigal who came home and the father put a ring on his finger, shoes on his feet, and a robe around his shoulders to honor him in celebration of His beloved son's return. So, Shulamite and Solomon celebrated their renewed fellowship and love.

And then, with great anticipation, we journeyed with them through the Judean wilderness, then northward along the Jordan River, through the Bet Shean Pass, until we arrived in the Galilee, Shulamite's home.

Here in Shulamite's home, we met her friends and family. We are introduced to her little sister and older brothers. We listened as Shulamite sang and danced for her loved ones. And then, so like Shulamite, as she was singing, she playfully led her beloved Solomon away to the scented slopes over yonder and engaged in sweet romance and intimacy under the tree. The very same apple tree where they first met, the very same place where they first fell in love. Thus ends this beautiful love story.

The Song of Songs reminds us of Christ's love for His bride, the Church. It reminds us how He longs for sweet intimate fellowship and communion. It reminds us of the great price Jesus paid because of His never-ending love for us.

This Song points us to the cross of Calvary and to the empty tomb. The Song of Songs leads us to the splendor and glory of heaven's pleasures and beauty. The story of Shulamite and Solomon also reminds us of the importance of communication, understanding, and romantic intimacy between husband and wife. It clearly defines that husband and wife are to complement and complete each other.

The Song teaches us that God ordained marriage and put His stamp of approval upon it. That a man and a woman should not simply dwell together and live together in the same home, but through ceremony, recognizing God as the designer of marriage, come together in Holy Matrimony.

This Song of Songs brings us to a clear understanding that only Christ, our heavenly Beloved, can fill the void in our lives. That only Christ can bring fulfillment, joy, and true pleasure. That only when a couple puts Christ at the center of their lives will they find true purpose, meaning, and direction. For without our beloved Christ, we can do nothing (John 15:5).

The Song of Songs also prods us to a greater understanding of Christian principles:

No relationship is more important than your relationship with the Lord Jesus Christ.

Nurture that relationship, treasure it, build it, pray about it, and affirmatively plan on how you can enhance it (Matt. 22:37, 38; Rev. 2:4–5).

Seek the approval of God rather than trying to please men (Gal. 1:10).

Fear God, not men (Ps. 27:1; 33:8; 56:11; 118:6–9; Prov. 29:25; Ex. 15:11; 20:18–20; Gen. 22:12; Lev. 11:44–45).

Take comfort that the Holy Spirit Himself is praying for you, as is our precious Lord Jesus Christ Himself interceding for you (Rom. 8:26, 34).

Realize that God has a purpose for your life. Find that purpose then do it for the glory of God.

Romans 8:28 is not just a pretty or trite saying. It is one of the most practical, bedrock, faith-enhancing verses in all of Scripture. Know this verse, believe it, and practice it in your own heart.

Be wise about what is good, and innocent about what is evil (Rom. 16:19; Jer. 4:22).

In your speech to others, speak only what is helpful for building others up (Eph. 4:29).

Be excited about the reality that the Holy Spirit lives in you; that the Holy Spirit abides with you always; that the Holy Spirit always has His hands of help and comfort ready; that the Holy Spirit Himself will teach you spiritual wisdom from the Scripture; and that the Holy Spirit Himself will guide your mind and heart as you plan for the day and for the days to come. Remembering these benefits, therefore, do not grieve or put out the Holy Spirit's fire in your life (1 Thess. 5:19; Eph. 4:30–32; Ps. 139:7–10; 1 Cor. 2:10–11; Acts 1:8; Rom. 15:19; John 14:26; Acts 9:31; John 14:16–17; John 16:8; Rom. 8:11; 1 Cor. 6:19; Rom. 5:5; Lk. 12:12; 1 Cor. 2:10–16; Jude 20; 1 John 4:1–6; Rom 8:9; 14:17; 15:16).

Always trust in God to keep His promises (1 Thess. 5:24; Ezek. 36:36).

Be careful about your thought life (2 Cor. 10:5). The Lord would not give us a command if He did not give us the ability to obey by His grace.

If you ever have a need, ask God, and in your asking, ask with right motives (James 4:2–3).

If you every feel unloved, meditate on the spiritual promise and reality: *The eternal God is your refuge, and underneath are the everlasting arms* (Deut. 33:27).

Because God is the rock eternal, you can have unwavering trust and perfect peace (Isa. 26:3, 7, 12).

Anger, bitterness, fear, and worry are all self-inflicted grief (1 Peter. 5:7; Matt. 6:25–34).

God does not want you to fret. God does not allow you to be a worrier.

Do not be anxious; do not worry. Jesus said, Do not worry about your life . . . who of you by worrying can add a single hour to his life? Oh you of little faith . . . Do not worry . . . Do not worry about tomorrow.

Remember, you decide by your choices and by your obedient affirmative actions whether you will be an instrument for noble purposes and whether your life will be effective and productive (2 Tim. 2:20, 21; 2 Peter 1:5–9).

To live on the cutting edge for God, you must be willing to take steps forward with the eyes of faith (2 Cor. 5:7).

Life is short. It is merely a breath, and it will be over. By contrast, eternity is forever. Walk in this brief life in light of eternity, and fight the good fight (1 Tim. 1:18; 2 Tim. 4:7).

It is good to realize this profound truth: *I can't . . . God can* (2 Cor. 3:4–6; John 15:5; Phil. 4:13).

God expects you to put into practice what you learn from the Word. Get out of your chair, get out of the pew, and simply "do it" (James 1:22; Luke 8:21).

Keep short sin accounts with God. Confess it and make it right with the Lord (1 John 1:9, Heb. 9:14).

Remember, God is present, and He is watching (Prov. 5:21).

Ask yourself, "Am I becoming more and more conformed into the image of Christ?" (1 Cor. 1:7–8; Rom. 8:29)

Concerning your income and material possessions, be reminded that you are merely a steward. One hundred percent of what you earn is bought by God; one hundred percent of what you have is owned by God. Ask yourself, "How will I invest God's material resources for God's purposes and God's glory?"

Pray for missionaries (Rom. 15:30).

Christ is building His Church. You will not receive God's ultimate benefits and blessing from your local church unless you give of yourself and of your means to the local body. As a member of your church, work for peace and harmony so long as it is not a compromise of actual biblical truth (Ps. 133:1).

Do not accept or receive a bad report about a brother in the Lord. It is an act of hatred and disloyalty to assume a wrong motive about the acts of a brother in the Lord. Do not gossip about a Christian brother, and do not listen to someone who does. Do not serve as a magnet for malcontents or a clearing house for complainers (1 Cor. 13:4–8; Prov. 20:19; 25:23; Rom. 1:29; 2 Cor. 12:20; Ps. 34:13; John 3:5–12; Prov. 10:19; 13:3; 15:2; 17:14, 27; 21:23; 26:20–22).

Think of the splendor and glories of heaven. Think of being in the presence of God unfettered of this sinful flesh. For a Christian to fear death is an absolute insult to God and to the sacrifice of Jesus Christ which gave us our glorious salvation and eternal life.

God made you who you are by His divine plan and with the fullness of His divine power. God made no mistakes when He created certain limitations in you. God made no mistakes when He gave you talents and gifts. Never lament God's design, and always seek to invest and use for God's purposes and glory those special strengths, qualities, gifts, and talents which God gave to you and constructed in you to make you special and unique.

Make Christ the center in your life and your home. Be a faithful and fruitful ambassador for our precious Savior (Lk. 19:5, 6; Eph. 4:31–32; 5:1, 2; 2 Cor. 5:17–20).

Gentlemen, you are the High Priest of the home. You must lift the banner of Christ high for your family. As you lift Christ up, as He is center in your life and your home, you and your wife weave together a beautiful tapestry of love, honor, peace, and harmony. Like Solomon, you lead, protect, provide for, cherish, and love your wife. You embrace her with a passion and love her endlessly, giving of yourself even unto death.

Ladies, like Shulamite, open your heart and life to your beloved. You are the queen of your home. You bring music, dancing, and joy. You work willingly with your hands and seek wool and flax. "[Your] children rise up and call [you] blessed; and [your] husband also, and he praises [you]" (Prov. 31:28). Your fear of the Lord brings you great beauty, praise, and honor.

As the two of you bring Christ into the braid of your life, as He is woven into the center, the Scripture says, "Though one may be overpowered by another, two can withstand him, [But] a three-fold cord is not quickly broken" (Eccl. 4:12). Alone, you are vulnerable. Together, you find a little more strength, but with Christ in the center of it all, you are strong, and you will be able to stand the onslaught of the trials and the testing that life brings. You will find joy, purpose, fulfillment, and direction when Jesus takes you by the hand and walks you across the street. He will carry you, protect you, watch over you, and care for your every need. He not only cares for your every need, but He will bless you profoundly—if not here, then over yonder on heaven's shores.

Either way, with Christ, you have all you need; with Christ, you have love. With Christ, you have joy. With Christ, you have purpose. With Christ, you have peace. With Christ, you have victory. Christ is all and in all. Without Christ, you have nothing. Christ is all you need. This is the message of the Song of Songs.

Bibliography

Field, David. *Marriage Personalities*. Eugene, OR: Harvest, 1985.

Fruchtenbaum, Arnold G. *Biblical Lovemaking, A Study of the Song of Solomon*. Ariel Ministries, 1983.

Goldman, Alex J. *The Eternal Books Retold*. Northvale, NJ: Aronson, 1999.

Henry, Matthew. *Matthew Henry's Commentary*. Peabody, MA: Hendrickson, 2008.

Hubbard, David. *Mastering the Old Testament: Ecclesiastes, Song of Solomon*. Nashville: Word, 1991.

Ironside, H. A. *Proverbs, Song of Solomon*. Neptune, NJ: Loizeaux, 1981.

Lash, Jamie. *A Kiss A Day*. Hagerstown, MD: Ebed, 1996.

McGee, J. Vernon. *Poetry, Ecclesiastes and Song of Solomon*. Nashville: Nelson, 1991.

Mead, Frank S. *Who's Who in the Bible*. Uhrichsville, OH: Barbour, 1986.

Nee, Watchman. *Song of Songs*. Fort Washington, PA: Christian Literature Crusade, 1965.

Phillips, John. *Exploring the Song of Solomon*. Neptune, NJ: Loizeaux, 1984.

Refior, Paul D. *It's your Choice, a Happy & God-honoring Marriage*. Warsaw, IN: Rafe, 1998.

Rice, John R. *The Home: Courtship, Marriage, and Children*. Murfreesboro, TN: Sword of the Lord, 1987.

Shepherd, David R., and Duane A. Garett. *Shepherd's Notes, Ecclesiastes, Song of Solomon*. Nashville: B. & H., 1998.

Spurgeon, C. H. *Treasury of David*. Nashville: Nelson, 1985.

Stanely, Scott. *Heart of Commitment: Cultivating Lifelong Devotion in Marriage*. Nashville: Nelson, 1998.

Swindoll, Charles R. *Strike the Original Match*. Portland, OR: Multnomah, 1980.

Trepp, Leo. *A History of the Jewish Experience, Eternal Faith, Eternal People*. New York: Behrman, 1973.

Walvoord, John F., and Roy B. Zuck. *Bible Knowledge Commentary: An Exposition of the Scriptures*. 2 vols. Wheaton, IL: Victor, 1985.

CPSIA information can be obtained
at www.ICGtesting.com
Printed in the USA
FSHW020656241020

9 781725 277632